COPING WITH PEER PRESSURE

LESLIE S. KAPLAN

THE ROSEN PUBLISHING GROUP, INC.

NEW YORK

Published in 1983, 1987 by The Rosen Publishing Group, Inc.
29 East 21st Street, New York, N.Y. 10010

Copyright 1983, 1987 by Leslie Schenkman Kaplan
Revised Edition 1987

Library of Congress Cataloging in Publication Data

Kaplan, Leslie S. (Leslie Schenkman)
  Coping with peer pressure.

  (Coping)
  Includes index
  I. Title.   II. Series: Coping (Rosen Publishing Group)
HQ796.K285   1983   305.2′35   82-23050
ISBN 0-8239-0768-6

Manufactured in the United States of America

About the Author

Leslie Schenkman Kaplan, EdD, is a Licensed Professional Counselor working primarily with adolescents. She knows young people through her active involvement as a high school guidance counselor, a peer counseling trainer, a hot-line consultant, and a private practitioner. Dr. Kaplan's articles on dealing with adolescents appear in national counseling journals, and she gives presentations on these topics at state and national conferences. She also teaches graduate counseling courses at the College of William and Mary in Williamsburg, Virginia, and parent education seminars for the Newport News Adult Education Office.

Originally from New York, Dr. Kaplan earned a BA degree in English from Rutgers University, an MA from Columbia University, an MS in Counseling from the University of Nebraska at Omaha, and a doctorate from the College of William and Mary.

A dedicated and concerned professional, Dr. Kaplan serves as an Independent Examiner for the Virginia Board of Professional Counselors' Licensure Examination, and on the editorial board of the Virginia Counselors Association *Journal*. She has twice been named Virginia Peninsula Counselor of the Year, 1980–81 and 1981–82.

Dr. Kaplan currently lives in Newport News with her husband, Dr. Michael L. Kaplan, a research meteorologist, and their son, Reid.

Acknowledgments

I offer special thanks to persons who gave me support and assistance while I was writing this book.

I want to thank my husband, Michael L. Kaplan, for offering a model of creativity, determination, and plain hard work in his own life. Most important, though, I thank him for having the courage to allow me to express myself.

I gratefully thank Scott Holland, Mary Whitaker, and Elizabeth Zoby for helping to develop more fully my ideas about gifted adolescents. They are certainly among the most talented and interesting young people I know.

To Gaye Todd Adegbalola, Richard "Pop" Pitts, and JoAnn Turner, I offer sincere appreciation for sharing their rich perspectives about how peer pressure affects black youths. They enabled me to understand more sensitively.

I thank Jayne Easley, Lisa Hall, Charles O. "Chuck" Matthews, April Wells, and Elizabeth Zoby for their patient reading of the manuscript and their incisive comments about its authenticity, thoroughness, and clarity.

To all the young people who trusted me enough to let me know them, I give deepest thanks. This is their story.

Contents

Foreword   ix

I. *Adolescence: A Process of Transition*   1
A Time of Uncertainty
Adolescence: The Years
Adolescence: The Process
Role of the Peer Group
How Peer Groups Change During
    Adolescence
The Peer Group's Values
Living with Teenagers

II. *Peer Pressure in Adolescence*   23
What Is Peer Pressure?
Reasons Why Adolescents Give In to Peer
    Pressure
A Model: How Individuals Experience Peer
    Pressure
Areas of Peer Pressure
Peer Counselors
"Just Say No"

III. *Peer Pressure, Achievement, and Adventure*   57
Adolescent Need for Achievement
The Lure of Adventure
Peer Pressure as Scapegoat
Learning Leadership
Conclusion

IV. *Adolescent Sexuality*   84
The Role of Sexuality in Adolescence
Adolescent Sexuality as Exploratory
  Behavior
Why Adolescents Become Sexually Active
Peer Pressure and Adolescent Sexuality
Role of Peers in Understanding
  Sexuality
Conclusion

V. *Adolescents and Loss*   111
What Is Loss?
Loss: A Special Problem for Adolescents
Types of Loss During Adolescence
Role of Friends in Romantic Breakup
Conclusion

VI. *Peer Pressure and Special Populations*   147
Gifted Adolescents and Peer Pressure
Learning-disabled and Peer Pressure
Minorities and Peer Pressure
Conclusion

VII. *Independence and Responsibility*   184
Ways to Move Beyond Peer Pressure
Positive Peer Pressure
Conclusion

Index   203

Chapter I

Adolescence: A Process of Transition

A Time of Uncertainty

Adolescence today is a complicated and difficult enterprise. Both the individuals and the world in which they find themselves are changing.

Young people face a situation in which social and cultural expectations are shifting. From duty and responsibility of the 1950's and early '60's, to "Me first!" in the late 1960's and '70's, to still different values in the 1980's, we see our society in rapid change. Many parents experienced these changes during their own lifetimes, and they are uncertain whether the values and ideas with which they were raised still work for their children. More choices for thought and action exist now than ever before, but fewer bases for making decisions about these alternatives remain. The former solid beliefs that if a person did A, B, and C, then D, E, and F would follow are gone. Confusion, uncertainty, and complexity remain.

In the late twentieth century, no clear-cut signs mark a dependent child separate from an independent adult. Yet the child must gradually learn how to think and act responsibly. Young people must learn how to live in their changing bodies, must learn the skills to develop and keep friends, must learn to understand themselves and act responsibly, and must make important decisions about their futures. Unfortunately, the only honest answer for their questions about how they will be able to know and face all these expectations is, "It depends."

"Is my body the right shape and size to be considered attractive?"

"How can I one day become deeply involved with another person when today I do not even have the confidence to start a conversation with anyone?"

"How can I learn what I really feel and think when I feel a great pounding tightness throughout my chest whenever I even start to figure it out?"

"What career can I plan for today that I will enjoy, be successful at, and have a job waiting for me in seven or more years when I'm ready to go to work?"

"How will I be able to become a well-trained, respected professional and still have a chance for a fulfilling family life?"

"It depends . . ."

An adult's vague answers seem very unnerving and unsatisfying. Why begin preparing today when no guarantees exist about tomorrow's payoff? Peer groups provide the questioning adolescent with more immediate, concrete, and satisying answers than can a concerned parent or an objective, unrelated adult. Although the reassurance gained by a peer's answers may be short-lived, effective for several weeks or years, at least the answers give a basis for moving ahead. Only by interacting with the environment and seeing what happens can adolescents begin to develop and refine the attitudes and skills they will need for a competent and satisfying adulthood.

Adolescence: The Years

Adolescence is a time of transition. The young person is neither a helpless child nor a fully responsible, mature adult. Adolescence is both a period of time and a series of separate yet related processes.

In part, adolescence means a period of time. Some observers divide the period into three stages covering the years from ages eleven to seventeen and beyond. Early adolescence, ages eleven to fourteen, brings the immediate response to puberty's physical and hormonal changes. Young people spill over with energy and intensity, switch moods, behave unpredictably, and develop a new ability to think abstractly about things they never personally experienced. Their bodies' new dimensions awe and confuse them. Many become very self-conscious, thinking only of themselves. Individuals wonder about who they are becoming, and groups of adolescents wonder about who they are.

Middle adolescence, ages fifteen to seventeen, brings more complex and subtle ways of relating to others. Young people become more at ease with their physical selves and think about building relationships and practicing new skills. They make choices about when to be part of the group and when to act apart from it.

From age seventeen onward, late adolescence lasts until an indefinite future point when the individuals behave responsibly, knowing and accepting themselves as unique persons. Older adolescents are able to make major choices about life's work and begin acting to make their lives move forward in desirable ways. These persons have also learned how to start and sustain meaningful personal relationships.

Adolescence: The Process

Adolescence means more than a set of years. It becomes a process of changes and developments in several areas. The central task of all adolescent growth is self-definition. Self-definition occurs in physical, social, and psychological areas of the young persons' lives.

Adolescence includes the actual physical changes of growing as well as learning to live in these new bodies. The inches added to arms and legs, the new musculature in the chest and back make people feel different just walking through space. Yesterday's clothing doesn't fit, of course, but the new physique undoes the individual's entire relationship to the world. Walking feels strange. Reaching feels strange. Crossing a familiar bedroom means suddenly bumping into the desk or chair that never seemed to get in the way before. It means tapping one's feet continuously whenever seated. It means a new intense interest in privacy.

A new body comes with and responds to new internal equipment. Hormones and endocrine messages for aggressiveness and sexuality bring problems at first. Young people experience their insistent, seemingly overpowering strength without warning of its onset or understanding how to manage it. As a youngster in grammar school, a girl might have felt annoyed if another person got in her way; now the feeling seems more like anger, and she wants to strike out sharply in rage. Many a fourteen-year-old boy has clutched his desk and silently prayed for quick and total invisibility because he feared standing up in class to answer the teacher's math question: he risked overwhelming embarrassment if his classmates noticed his arousal.

Along with the new body and its chemical endowment come the social expectations of what it means to be a person of a particular gender in this culture. Recent laws and social opinion have altered the ways in which men and women are "supposed to" behave. Careers once closed to all except one small segment of the population are now open to all persons with the necessary interests and skills. Male nurses and female engineers, for example, are no longer isolated pioneers in their fields. Likewise, girls can now phone boys and ask them out to the movies without being automatically laughed at or called "fast" or "weird."

Nevertheless, while the headlines say, "No difference!" the truth is quite different. Adolescents learn their sex roles by watching adults around them. They have watched since they were young children. Parents and other adults teach children how men and women ought to behave. Now as thinking young people, they must either act on the learning or change it in ways that agree with their own view of the world.

Each adolescent asks, "Who am I, physically?"

Social expectations also change with adolescence. Young people begin moving away from total reliance on family for day-to-day decision-making or for emotional and financial support. They move toward increasing independence and personal mastery of new situations. Mother used to be able to shop for her child's September wardrobe in a morning's trip to one department store. Now she and her newly assertive adolescent spend days and miles selecting the right fashions. In addition, adolescents press their rights to choose their own friends, music, and recreation. They often want the chance to solve their own problems with teachers and complain, insulted, when their concerned parents offer to step in. Just yesterday, parental involvement would have been gratefully welcomed, but today it is humiliating. Frequently, teenagers hold after-school jobs and accept responsibility for budgeting their time and money. Moreover, in times of crisis or confusion, adolescents turn first to their friends for support, understanding, and advice. Parents are no longer the only resources in their adolescents' lives.

Much learning about people also occurs during this time. Young people begin developing deep and meaningful relationships with friends of the same sex. They learn how to accommodate others, when to give, when to take, and how. They learn loyalty, trust, empathy, and confidentiality through shared experiences, trials, and celebrations. They learn which behaviors are acceptable and which are not. Developing satisfying heterosexual relationships brings more new skills to master.

Each adolescent asks, "Who am I, socially?"

Again during this time, young people must begin to find a vocational direction for themselves. Until adolescence, school year followed school year in unending sequence. Now the adolescents must look ahead, identify a life's purpose, and find a way to reach it. Adolescents must move from fantasizing about building bridges to assessing personal interests and abilities. They must tentatively explore alternative courses of action that take these interests, abilities, and life situations into account. They must then make a plan to put these decisions into action.

Each adolescent asks, "Who am I, vocationally?"

Adolescence includes the psychological changes that come with the mature body and the new social expectations. Young people experience an increased emotionality that alternately whispers and roars. A C grade on a term paper may lead to several days' depression and self-doubt for the high-achieving student. Receiving praise from a favorite teacher may lead another student to a wonderful feeling of importance and smug satisfaction. Adolescents invented "Cloud 9" and "the pits."

This phase of a young person's life upsets regular behavior in many ways. The familiar habits of thinking and acting are either no longer available or suddenly do not work well. The old ways don't fit, but new, more appropriate methods have yet to be developed. A problem at school used to mean asking Mom or Dad to call the teacher for a solution. No longer is this a face-saving alternative. One group of girls once valued boys either for a fast game of softball or simply to ignore. Now that friends expect to begin dating, they openly ridicule this old approach. A helpless, confused feeling results as a comfortable style of life gives way. The uneasy feelings last until more effective attitudes or behaviors can be tested and found satisfactory. With so many questions and so few answers immediately available, adolescents experience anxiety and stronger, more pressing emotions than ever before.

Other physiological factors including diet and rest enter the picture. A junk-food diet or an extracurricular afternoon coupled with a homework-until-2 A.M. regimen, so typical of many adolescents, contributes to the body's inability to soothe or understand emotional tension. Poor nourishment and fatigue often lead to poor decisions and bad moods.

Something else contributes to the psychological changes occurring in adolescence. New ways of thinking and new ways of organizing thought begin. Piaget and Inhelder[1] note that adolescent thinking differs radically from a child's thinking. The adolescent gradually becomes able to impose structure and put together once separate bits of information into a whole that makes sense. This results from interaction of the maturing nervous system and brain components with a demanding social and educational environment. The outcome is the ability to imagine possibilities not present in one's own daily experience, to fantasize present and future choices, to blend facts and thoughts and arrive at novel conclusions.

With these new intellectual skills, identifying personal motives and values, understanding others, weighing the

---

[1] Piaget, Jean, and Inhelder, Barbel, *The Growth of Logical Thinking. From Child to Adolescence* (New York: Basic Books, 1958).

impact others have on themselves, playing with abstract ideas, and deciding on a life plan suddenly become possible for thought, review, and action. Teenagers can now criticize their own thinking. They can think about thought. They can begin planning realistically for their own future and supporting attractive ideologies or political movements based on complex ideas.

This new form of intelligence makes the transition to adulthood easier by allowing young people to plan for and practice playing adult roles. Adolescents develop aware leadership styles and effective social skills, and they practice helpful worker habits. As a result, adolescents can experience many new emotions. They can make more choices and take more actions. Young people see what happens in their lives and ask, "What does it mean to me?" Since intelligence and emotions are part of the same personality, the more things about which individuals think, the more they will feel different experiences with their emotions.

Each adolescent asks, "What does this idea or experience or feeling tell me about who I am?"

Role of the Peer Group

Young people are only partially aware of the many expectations facing them on the way to maturity. They must master an enormous number of tasks. It is no wonder that most adolescents do not know exactly what must be done or even how to begin. What steps enter into moving from being school children with almost all needs met by parents or teachers to becoming adults with self-understanding and with the attitudes and skills needed to accept full responsibility for themselves? What happens when young people feel the social pressure to act like adults with their mature bodies but inside still feel like silly kids without the information or chances to behave in truly mature ways? How do adolescents come to terms with the need to be different from their parents, independent and unique, as well as with the real fear of losing the emotional and financial support that they still need?

Not only are the expectations for adolescents unclear, but so are the ways of reaching them. One young person comments, "I feel the pressures and tensions inside me, but I don't know where they're coming from. Every time I start to look more closely, my palms start sweating and my heart beats so fast that I become frightened. I just can't seem to make decisions about anything, and so often I'm only a few breaths away from panic." This description holds true for many.

On the other hand, when the expectations for adolescents become clearly known, the way ahead opens. It is helpful when parents, teachers, guidance counselors, older siblings, or friends take the time to clarify young people's concerns and help them see possible solutions. Trial and error can then move them closer by steps, half-steps, and occasional missteps to the desired ends. For instance, young people need to hear that choosing a career is not like pin-the-tail-on-the-donkey. It is not an all-or-nothing, now-or-never proposition. Instead it is a series of small decisions. With this background they can develop the proper attitude of looking at their choices and trying them out. They can first focus on their own interests and abilities and select those academic or extracurricular experiences that will broaden and deepen them. They can begin the process of understanding themselves better and looking for resources to help them. Young people then take one step at a time. They make one small decision at a time.

With clear expectations, adolescents can set their own goals and begin acting to meet them. Their growth and maturity then become an ongoing sequence of events. Many adolescents who clearly understand what they want to accomplish can actively participate in creating their own meaning and identities.

Unfortunately, most of the tasks adolescents must master remain unclear. Some seem mystifying, such as, "How do I get from geometry class in high school to becoming an electrical engineer?" Others seem unreachable, such as, "How will I ever get married when I am so uncomfortable in my own body and become tongue-tied speaking with members of the opposite sex?" When the expectations for behavior are unknown or unclear, young people feel pressure to act without really understanding how or where or why. Discomfort and anxiety result.

This anxious feeling is very unpleasant, so some young people act simply to get rid of the uneasy rumbling. They can adopt a strategy of extreme caution, withdrawal, or denial. Many say they'll deal with that troubling issue tomorrow, maybe. Others insist that no problem exists. Everything is fine. A different strategy involves acting rashly and impulsively. Taking action, any action, no matter how effective or useless it may be in the long run, feels better than waiting and allowing the internal tension to build still greater. To some adolescents, not acting means looking as if they are not in control of the situation. At least doing something at once gets rid of the tension for the moment. Thinking ahead or planning a long-term solution becomes too expensive. Waiting costs calm and costs looking decisive to those watching.

Feeling anxious because one does not know how or when or why to respond deeply troubles young people. Under this tension they feel lonely and isolated. At the time in their lives when young people believe they are supposed to be taking charge of themselves, they feel small and confused. Even those adolescents who know what others' expectations are and how to meet them have no guarantees. They realize they might still fall on their faces at times, and this fact makes them more nervous. They want answers and solutions to reassure them. They want a way to feel in control of their own lives. Many young people find their concerns answered when they become members of a peer group.

Answering Concerns About Their Bodies Peer group membership answers adolescents' concerns about their bodies. Daily, adolescents secretly ask themselves, "Am I developing normally?" "My arms are too long. Does anyone else notice? Am I the only one with this problem?" "My ankles are too thin. Does anyone else notice? Am I the only one with this problem?"

Many physical changes occur during the ages eleven to fifteen. No wonder the individuals suspect that the new inches, muscles, or curves are too much, too little, too soon, or too late. Body proportions sometimes do shift out of sync for a time while the growth of one body part catches up with another.

Discussing these fears with other young people experiencing similar physical changes and asking similar questions about their impact helps adolescents to accept their physical development. In several ways, the group reassures the individuals that they are acceptable and not abnormal. First, the group provides chances for members to look openly at their concerns. They can question appropriate body types found in magazines, classmates, older siblings, or well-known personalities and compare these models to their own bodies. Favorable comparisons mean that the adolescents celebrate their good fortune. Unfavorable matchups lead to joking about the differences between the actual and the ideal, ridiculing the unattained muscles or inches, or inventing ways to cover up or avoid the difference. In any case, a group of individuals of the same gender finds the bodies of its members acceptable.

Next, the group offers occasions for silent comparisons. A young man who suspects his shoulders are not broad enough to be thought "manly" will have many chances to compare his shoulders to those of his friends, either on the basketball court, during gym class, or by studying their builds during an after-the-game pizza. The teenage girl who is sensitive about her ample hips will have the chance to do some silent judging of her own when she is with her friends.

Peer groups can help adolescents accept their physical development by devising means to hide it. Body differences appear less different when people dress alike. Each group has its own look, from sophisticated dressy, to designer labels, to ratty jeans and T-shirts, to whatever is handy. Each group presents an identifiable image through a style of dressing that clearly states what is acceptable. This dress code can take the guesswork out of being clothed. For persons uncomfortable with themselves and their bodies and who dread the idea of being singled out for attention, a no-risk wardrobe means no failure. For the preppy group, for example, bib overalls, painter's pants, alligator shirts, and brass-initial bags are always acceptable.

For others, the unisex look meets a real need. Ill at ease with the expected male or female role, they find that the more ambiguous the look (regarding gender), the fewer the sexual expectations. Adolescents mask both male and female physiques with baggy overalls and full flannel shirts. Fewer people will advance the idea of romance to adolescent girls dressed in Mickey Mouse T-shirts, too-big wrap-around skirts, and scuffed oxfords. The body may say, "Mature Adult Here," but if the personality is not ready for the mature adult experience, the body will often wait disguised in unassuming clothes until it is.

Answering Social Concerns Becoming a peer group member meets many adolescent concerns about social expectations. Young people need to develop independence from their parents. They need to learn decision-making skills and the personal mastery to act on their own and live with the consequences. But young teenagers find these goals confusing, the ways of achieving them unclear. They feel dependent on their parents because they privately know that they lack the confidence and skills to succeed on the outside alone. Adolescents, however, deeply resent this need as a sign of weakness, often covering it up with bravado, arguments, and impulsive behavior.

Adolescents know that they must be different from their parents. For them, this is an important matter of self-esteem. They believe they must view the world differently than do their elders, and react differently to it as well. They know what they must move away from, yet they remain uncertain about what they must move toward. They need to develop new identities to define themselves. The peer group provides temporary aliases. For the present, at least, all others will know who they are: they are members of This Group.

The peer group defines what is "normal" for its members. The group defines "normal" attitudes, "normal" thoughts, "normal" behavior. Should the young person value education? The peer group has the answer. How should the young person solve a particular problem? The

peer group has the answer. Should the young person become sexually active on a first date? The peer group has
that answer, too.

Every peer group defines normalcy in attitude, thought,
and action in its own ways. Whatever the question, the
group has an answer. Then the trade-off begins. Each person gets something in the exchange. Adolescents gain
passports. They receive guides to living that help them
move beyond dependence on parents or family without
losing the emotional support of important others in life.
The peer code clearly spells out how to meet many of the
expectations placed on young people. Follow these rules
and you cannot fail in your peers' eyes. Wear these clothes,
act this way, do these things, and the group guarantees
your acceptance. In this manner, young people gain self-
esteem from separating from parents, a set of directions to
help avoid looking foolish or alone, and acceptance and
affection from loyal confederates.

On the other hand, the peer group also gains. Each new
member's following the code and accepting the group's
influence strengthens the code and verifies the correctness
of all the other members. Conformity for many adolescents
is not a price, costing individuality, but is a blessing,
freeing them from responsibility, loneliness, and possible
failure. All reinforce each other, person and group gaining
in the bargain.

Answering Concerns About Personal Worth   In addition, becoming a peer group member addresses many adolescents' concerns about their personal worth. As young
people begin emotionally separating from their parents, they
risk feeling alone and helpless in a complex, fast-paced
world. Membership in a group means that the individuals
are acceptable, worthwhile, even lovable. Having friends

with whom to share secrets, fears, and adventures strengthens the adolescents' sense of their own value. They relish the social support and experience a new sense of personal mastery. They now know who they are, what they believe, and how they should behave. Group membership smooths the transition away from parental control toward becoming their own person.

How Peer Groups Change During Adolescence

A young person's circle of friends evolves during the years from early to late adolescence. Just as the individuals' needs and behaviors change with increasing experience and maturity, so, too, does the nature of their peer groups.

Dunphy [2] studied the makeup of adolescent cliques and crowds. A clique refers to a smaller group than a crowd, usually numbering from two to nine members. Clique members share intimate relationships and spend much time together. Members share similar values, tastes, interests, and moral views. They exchange ideas and secrets and accept each other as persons. They show much less openness and tolerance of outsiders' views. Members often come from the same socioeconomic background and are in the same grade at school, further reinforcing their similarities.

Alternately, crowds vary from fifteen to thirty members, and they often consist of several cliques coming together for shared activities. With the larger crowd size, as compared to the clique, organized social events become possible. This largeness, on the other hand, makes the forming of intimate relationships more difficult. There are more

[2] Dunphy, D. C., "The Social Structure of Urban Adolescent Peer Groups," *Sociometry 26,* (1963) 230–246, as cited in Coleman, John C., "Friendship and the Peer Group in Adolescence," Joseph Adelson, ed., *Handbook of Adolescent Psychology* (New York: John Wiley & Sons, 1980).

people to know but less time or fewer occasions to get involved with all.

Crowds offer a real advantage over cliques. The larger membership gives a way for moving from the one-sex group of early adolescence to the boy-girl relationships of later adolescence. Crowds offer chances for clique members to spend time with more individuals, male and female.

In early adolescence, boys tend to choose other boys as friends while girls select other girls. Chaperones at a middle school dance often find the boys lined up in pairs or trios along one wall, talking to each other, appearing not to be interested in the music or in the girls standing in the other half of the gym. Girls socialize among themselves across the room. Sometimes adults have difficulty starting the mixing, even though the adolescents have come to do just that.

The next group stage arrives when John's clique consents to attend a party hosted by Elise's clique. While friends still spend most of their energies with their close friends inside the clique, they enjoy talking with interesting people from a different group. Their social circle expands, and they begin learning new interpersonal skills that speed up this process. Fred thinks he doesn't know how to talk to girls and feels uneasy around them; but he is invited to Elise's party. He will figure out a way to go and make the best of it. Next time it will be easier.

In middle adolescence, boys and girls begin pairing off for short romances or for boy-girl friendships. Frequently, clique members who date or go steady earn their friends' respect. Boy-girl relationships symbolize adulthood, and adolescents value them. Sometimes boy-girl relationships start even before the individuals involved know how to begin or keep an intimate relationship. This situation leads to pairs coming together for days or weeks, breaking off communication, and either rejoining their close friends or forming new boy-girl pairs.

Meanwhile, the most respected and valued friends begin forming a new heterosexual clique. John and Elise, Mary Ellen and Charles, Pam and Mark often go to the movies or school dances as a group of couples. They have all been friends since fourth grade, and the boys played Little League baseball together.

This stage of group development allows the closeness of the one-sex clique as well as the boy-girl involvement. It presents a situation filled with chances for learning social skills and for brewing arguments among friends. As Elise begins spending more time with John and her couples friends, her former girlfriend, Sue, starts questioning Elise's loyalty to the girls' group. Unless Elise's old girlfriends also begin dating, they may feel resentment toward her and her apparent lack of interest in finding time to spend with them.

Not all cliques, however, look for involvement in boy-girl activities. Some young people do not want to begin dating yet. Others find that their deep involvement in hobbies or activities leaves few hours or little desire for relationships. Still others lack smooth social skills and cannot easily start or maintain a heterosexual relationship. Certain friendship groups choose to remain apart from boy-girl crowds. Since the larger society, however, values these relationships as preparation for adult roles, adolescents often feel pressured to get involved in a boy-girl relationship. As more alternative life-styles become available, adolescents will have more choices about when, how, and even whether they want to participate in these relationships.

In the fourth stage, adolescents become part of a fully

developed crowd. Many different boy-girl cliques interact in close association. This larger group organizes many social events for its members. They sit together at the prom and attend basketball games as a group.

By high school graduation, the real-world facts of out-of-town colleges, full-time jobs, and early marriages encourage the crowd's breakup. Some couples stay together. Other pairs separate to follow individual plans. Older individuals make their own directions as maturing young adults, less in need of the group membership benefits. They still have friendships, but they rely more on themselves than on their friends to make decisions and plans.

Peer groups change with the maturing needs of adolescents. Groups provide opportunities to develop intimate, empathic relationships. These groups, small and large, offer a testing ground for trying out new ways of behaving and dealing with people, and chances to share deeply one's most secret thoughts and feelings. Groups offer chances to give kindness and support to troubled friends and to learn how to be with persons very different in some ways from oneself.

The Peer Group's Values

Peer group membership has much to offer adolescents.[3] It is no wonder that young people want to belong.

First, peer groups help adolescents establish an identity apart from their parents. Friends provide a sense of belonging, acceptance, and approval to persons beginning to separate emotionally from the only security they have ever known. A full emotional life now exists for young people outside their families. Friends and strangers alike recog-

[3] Wagner, Hilmar, "The Increasing Importance of the Peer Group During Adolescence," *Adolescence* 6 (1971, Spring): 53–58.

nize them as unique persons, not merely as sons or daughters, brothers or sisters. Acceptance offered by the group makes young people feel okay about themselves. They belong, therefore they are normal and worthwhile.

Second, peer groups offer adolescents chances to develop important social skills. Young people learn to get along with others who are different from themselves. They develop empathy and appreciation of another person's experiences. Likewise, adolescents practice new roles and try out new behaviors. Now they can be leader, follower, or co-worker. In social events, adolescents carry out others' directions; at other times, these same young people take the lead in academic areas. Some become the foremost baseball players, while at other times they act as go-fers and collaborators in decorating the gym for Homecoming. In these ways, young people learn the types of acceptable and unacceptable behaviors, which styles win favor with others and which do not. They test leadership roles and followership roles. Through all, they test and refine their skills in many different activities.

Third, adolescents find that participating as peer group members brings many opportunities to learn an effective decision-making style. They have chances to put their beliefs and values into concrete action. They must look at the goal and find different ways to reach it, then choose which path to follow. Young people gradually understand how to connect thoughts and actions into successful, constructive behavior.

In addition, peer groups help adolescents establish values, attitudes, and behaviors in many areas of life. Choices of friends, clothing, dating practices, and recreation, as well as solitary, reflective activities become areas for peer input. Through their unwritten rules and clear expectations, peer groups present a model for thought and behavior that the members consider appropriate to follow. The group creates an entire life-style for its members. Such rules help individuals who need to separate from family but are not yet ready to be totally self-directed.

Next, the group offers frequent occasions for blowing off steam. Members share their deepest concerns and fears with others who really understand. Openly expressing their troubles to others relieves a great deal of tension and reduces feelings of loneliness and strangeness. It also helps listeners to identify strongly with each other, fostering increased empathy and loyalty. Sharing experiences in this way also increases the amount of information or alternative solutions available to help solve these difficult situations.

Finally, peer group involvement helps build confidence among members in their collective and individual abilities to influence their own environments. Peers have more realistic and immediately reachable standards than do most adults in their lives. When adolescents discover that they can meet their friends' expectations, they build self-esteem. Success within the peer group during adolescence nurtures their confidence in themselves. In the near future, most of these young people will extend their reach beyond the group limits as they become independent young adults.

Living with Teenagers

Adolescence is a time of many changes. Change is often upsetting, even if it is for the better. Teens don't always like the changes they go through because they feel strange like their old selves. They think everyone is looking at them and laughing at their longer arms or new womanly shape. Teachers don't always like the changes because their teenage students are sometimes moody or restless, ready to cry, shout, or sulk when the day becomes too much for them to take.

Parents don't always like the changes, either. Teens become familiar strangers living in their homes. The young people don't look or act the way they did a few years back. What is more, parents who were viewed as all-knowing and all-powerful by their elementary-school children are now seen as stupid, old-fashioned, or mean by their teenagers. That steep drop in status in their children's eyes really hurts parents. Many nurse their wounded feelings by looking for every mistake teens make and using them as reasons for clamping down harder. Finding fault with their teens make adults feel more needed and more in charge.

Wise and caring adults, however, look past the teenage behavior they see. Wise and caring adults see the strange wardrobe and way-out hairdos and think, instead, of the young person's first attempts to be independent of the family. Such tries at being different from parents also represent attempts to decide for themselves which styles and values are important to them and which are just surface issues of little importance.

Wise and caring adults hear the endless arguing and nit-picking of adolescents and see instead efforts to use their new ability to think abstractly and about the future as well as to define and test a personal value system. These adults hear adolescent mumbling and think, instead, that here is a young person not yet confident enough about emerging ideas to say them loudly and clearly.

Wise and caring adults see adolescents acting silly with members of the opposite sex and realize that these young people are trying to learn to act as men and women. In the same vein, adults see that adolescents daydream because they have so many things in their lives to think about and plan for.

People who live and work with adolescents need to look past teenagers' annoying actions and see the positive ends at which they are aimed. Adolescents have much growing to do, and becoming a mature adult does not happen overnight. Recognizing the long, difficult passage from childhood to adulthood, adults who live and work with teens need to see mistakes in a different, more positive way.

Adolescent mistakes do happen. Teens do not do everything right the first, second, or even the third time they try. Adults make mistakes, too. But teens need to see their mistakes either as lack of learning or as errors of doing, not as signs of personal failure. Those who see weakness and failure will become fearful of growing as persons. Teens need to expect mistakes and not be afraid to try something new.

Unfortunately, teens want so much to appear mature and in control that they work very hard to cover up their mistakes or to avoid new, growth-producing situations in which they might not succeed. Rarely do they ask adults for help. Teens need sensitive adults in their lives to give them permission to err. They need positive adult guidance to look carefully at the mistakes to see what happened. What did they want to happen? What did happen? What part went right? What part went wrong? What would they do differently next time? When will they try the action with the new strategy? Reviewing, reflecting, and revising are the keys to good decision-making. Adults can help their teens develop this thoughtful and mature habit by using the teens' errors as the examples. In this way, teen mistakes can become positive tools to build better learning and better skills.

Peer Pressure in Adolescence

When a fifteen-year-old boy was asked why he drank beer during the high school basketball game despite the knowledge that such an activity violated school board and sheriff's policies, the youth replied, "All my friends do it." When a sixteen-year-old girl was asked why she rushed her dates out of the house before any conversation between the young man and her parents could begin, she commented, "All my friends do it that way." A parent tried to explain his fourteen-year-old son's arrest on a shoplifting charge, saying, "Jeff's a good kid. It's just all that peer pressure!"

Adolescents and adults frequently use peer influence as an explanation or a justification for their own or their teenagers' troubling behavior. Peer groups do gain importance during these years as young people seek the company of others like themselves. Friends provide a frame of reference, a set of beliefs and behaviors as they all begin their leave-taking from home. Adolescents increasingly spend time with others like themselves who offer support and understanding during the process of becoming young adults. Peer pressure is a popular catch-all phrase that deserves a closer look.

What Is Peer Pressure?

A group of persons who share similar values and circumstances influence each other's thoughts and behaviors.
The collective membership's beliefs become the group's
stand. For some, the group's position carries more weight
than the views of any individual members. Then the group's
beliefs seem forceful enough to persuade individual members to think and act as the group wants. Peer pressure
names this influence. For example, a certain group of young
people value meeting together before attending school
dances in order to make an impressive entrance. They encourage and expect the other members to join this activity.
They strongly disapprove when any member refuses to
come along.

Unlike formal clubs, the groups described in this book
do not have a definite membership list, a charter, or written by-laws. The membership remains more or less the
same with a degree of flexibility. Peer groups contain individuals who enjoy hanging out together. Occasionally
they invite "outsiders" to come along. Not all the friends
meet at the same time. The group does not elect a president or officers, but certain people's opinions seem to matter more than others' do. The rules exist informally.
Everyone knows what the friends expect regarding various
situations; if not, the friends quickly remind the uncertain
or the violators.

Peer pressure also means the attraction that prospective
and present group members feel toward a group's characteristics. These persons desire what the group offers. They
behave in ways that the group approves in exchange for
group membership. If the young people decide to meet
their friends for the predance preparations, they do so because they want the camaraderie, the sense of belonging,

the mutual support, and the recognition by outsiders that they are part of this group. Like the barter system, each party gives something so that each may receive something. When one party gives, the other feels pressure to give in return in order to uphold the contract. Similarly, adolescents feel pressure to give now in ways the group expects so that they will later receive what they want from the group.

Because peer groups give their members the qualities that young adults seek, these groups hold a very influential place in adolescent life. Groups offer independence from parents by providing an intimate personal life outside the family. They offer acceptance and approval from persons in the larger world and help young people feel confident and worthy. Groups offer social rules for interacting with others, thereby providing confused young people with acceptable guides for action and a sense of security. Groups hold out these goods in exchange for conformity and compliance with group demands.

For all adolescents' concern with personality and "being themselves," young people usually remain uncertain about their own priorities, goals, abilities, interests, feelings, and temperaments. Self-definition is their main work during this period in their lives. Answers come slowly through experience, evaluating how effective their efforts were, and revising their next approach. Learning these answers takes time, willingness to evaluate their own actions, opportunities to try new behaviors, increasing maturity of judgment, and skill. Meanwhile, young people often resist standing apart from group expectations. They either have not yet found their answers to who they are or how to deal with the world; or they lack the confidence to assert themselves and take a stand on these issues they have resolved.

Reasons Why Adolescents Give In to Peer Pressure

Many factors contribute to adolescents' tendency to give in to peer pressure. With uncertain identity and sense of personal worth, young people seek reassurance from going along with the crowd. Age, the reasons for joining a group, family influences, personal importance in the group, and the habit of blaming oneself all play roles.

Age and Peer Pressure   Several investigators [1] looked at the relationship between peer pressure and age in youths seven to twelve years old. The young people had to make a decision about the length of a line. They did not know that the other people in the room with them had secretly agreed beforehand to give the wrong answer. The researchers found that giving in to peer pressure was significantly related to age although not in a straightforward way. Children ages seven to nine showed a relatively low amount of conformity to peer pressure, while young people ages eleven to thirteen showed the most. Sensitivity to peer pressure gradually decreased after age thirteen. Other investigators agree with these findings.

Considering the complexities and uncertainties of their changing lives, it seems understandable that young adolescents in this study would give in to peer pressure more than would any other age group. In fact, these young people often seek peer group membership as an escape from the responsibility of acting on their own or the shame of doing only what their parents want them to do. Neither experience nor formal instruction has prepared young adolescents to make effective independent decisions about their own lives, yet they cannot continue to dependently

---

[1] Costanzo, P. R., and Shaw, M. E., "Conformity as a Function of Age Level," *Child Development 37* (1966): 967–975.

rely on their parents' judgments. For many, having the guidance of peer norms proves a blessing.

Motivation to Join a Group   The reasons why young people seek membership in a particular group affect the amount of influence the group will have in their lives. The motivation for belonging influences how readily they will give in to peer pressure.

Some researchers[2] suggest two motivational differences for joining and staying with a peer group. Many young people join the group mainly to gain information or access to opportunities that the group provides. Natalie wants to become part of the leadership clique in her school because she likes the prestige that this group carries. The newspaper and yearbook editors, class and student government officers belong. Teachers pay great respect to members, calling them by name in class or in the halls. Members seem to know how to make things happen. Natalie wants to join this group because it provides the opportunities she seeks.

On the other hand, other young people want group membership primarily for social and emotional support. They feel better simply by having others around. Bruce wants to become part of a clique that eats lunch together in the school yard, attends school activities as a group, and regularly listens to records at one member's house on weekends. These fellows seem at ease with one another and occasionally date attractive young women. Bruce feels uncomfortably alone, left out of enjoyable activities. Nothing seems meaningful because nothing is shared. He very much wants to have friends and belong.

If the group demands an antisocial act that does not sit

[2] Condry, John, and Siman, Michael L., "Characteristics of Peer and Adult Oriented Children," *Journal of Marriage and the Family 36* (1974, August): 543–554.

well with the young person's own values and beliefs, the individuals with different reasons for joining may respond in differing ways. Adolescents who join a group for information and access face an uneasy choice. They can follow their own judgment or follow the group's will. These young people, however, are more likely to leave the group and avoid the unwanted behavior than are those who joined for emotional support. The persons who belong mainly to gain the acceptance and approval of the members need to go along with the group more than they need to be true to their own values and beliefs. These individuals more readily give in to peer pressure. The peer pressure will be harder for Bruce than for Natalie to ignore.

Likewise, when young people who joined the group for information and opportunities begin finding their own, outside sources of information, or when the information they receive from the group becomes less helpful than it used to be, they may decide to leave the group altogether and act on their own. To persons belonging for emotional support, fear of rejection by the group upsets them more than even the inner anxiousness, dissatisfaction, and mixed feelings they experience about what they are doing. At least with the group they are not alone.

Family Influences   The family situation influences the reasons for seeking group membership and the readiness to give in to peer pressure. The same study[3] finds that families in which the parents express relatively little concern or affection for their growing children, show a "do whatever you want; I don't care" attitude, and apply rules inconsistently lead to young adolescents desperately needing approval and affection. If not gained from their par-

[3] Ibid.

ents, these young people will find approval and affection with their friends. They join a peer group feeling so dependent on keeping the group's acceptance and approval that they frequently follow its dictates sooner than would a member from a different type of family. Young people from families that show active concern, expect their children to meet certain standards of performance, enforce rules consistently, and encourage family members to try new experiences and put out their best efforts are not so dependent on keeping group approval. These latter young people often feel better about themselves as worthwhile and capable persons than do those from unconcerned families. They build confidence from opportunities in which they can successfully meet their parents' expectations. They learn at home that the environment responds in predictable ways, and they have a surety about their ability to master whatever comes. They frequently have the point of view and self-assurance to stand apart from group influence when they choose to do so.

Additional Influences   Adolescents' status within the group also affects how they will respond to peer pressure. Another research team[4] conducted an experiment to measure how group members rated each other's importance to the group in relationship to the member's readiness to give in to peer pressure. Young people in grades three, six, nine, and eleven participated in experiments. They decided which of two pictures they liked better. They were later told which picture a highly valued group member preferred. Results showed that members ranked lower by their friends were more willing to go along with peer influence than were members valued higher by the group.

[4] Harvey, O. J., and Rutherford, J., "Status in the Informal Group," *Child Development 31* (1960): 377–385.

It appears that adolescents judged by group members to be less important to the group as a whole are most susceptible to peer influence. Since they have a lesser value to the group, their continued membership and acceptance seem less secure than that of more important members. Perhaps the low-status persons suspect that if they don't go along with the opinion leaders or high-status members, they risk being cold-shouldered out of group activities. They lack confidence in their own opinions and prefer the security of following an important member's opinions.

From another perspective, perhaps the less valued group members receive less important status because they seem uncertain and lack their own clear-cut, confident opinions. They do not show the assertive leadership skills that contribute to high-status membership. Either way, these less valued group members become the most ready to give in to peer pressure.

The tendency to blame oneself for whatever goes wrong is another factor influencing susceptibility to peer pressure. Costanzo[5] included young people ages seven to twenty-one in a study investigating this dimension. The participants completed a story in which the hero accidentally caused a mishap or disaster. They then told who they thought was to blame. Results found those persons who tended to blame themselves for an accident were the same persons most likely to give in to peer pressure. Persons willing to shoulder all the responsibility for a mishap, justified or not, lack self-confidence and a good feeling about their own worth and abilities. Adolescents not valuing their own opinions or talents most readily give in to others' views.

[5] Costanzo, P. R., ''Conformity Development as a Function of Self-blame,'' *Journal of Social Psychology 14* (1970): 366–374.

A Model: How Individuals Experience Peer Pressure

Generally, this book uses the phrases "peer pressure" and "peer influence" as if they were the same thing. Peer pressure is the popular term and enjoys wide use in referring to the impact of the group's judgments on persons desiring to become or remain members of that group. The word "pressure," however, sounds like a negative force beyond the individuals' ability to overcome it. Investigators prefer the term "peer influence" because it seems more neutral. "Peer influence" simply describes what happens rather than evaluates it. Influence is what happens. Pressure is how it feels. Using these terms more precisely helps clarify how young people experience this dimension.

To adolescents with little solid sense of who they are or what they're worth, the peer group's expectation that the members think and behave in "appropriate" ways brings relief. Through group membership, the young people do not have to decide how to think or act. They do not risk possible failure or lonely isolation from others. The group provides the answers and the safety. To other adolescents with positive views of themselves and with better understanding of their own personalities and values, peer group expectations become simply more decisions to make. Sometimes the adolescents go along with the group if doing so will meet their present interests. Sometimes they decide that their best interests lie in saying "No!" to the group's plans.

Adolescents choose to join groups prepared to accept the group rules as their legitimate dues. This is the contract. Going along is the rate of exchange. Yet choice always exists. Nothing is forced, although sometimes it feels as though it is. The experience of peer influence varies importantly among individuals.

Table 1

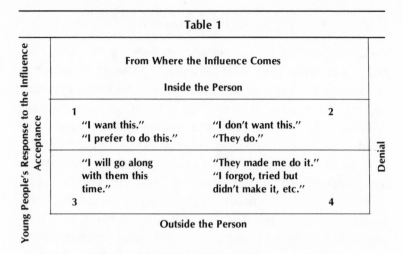

		From Where the Influence Comes	
		Inside the Person	
	1		2
	"I want this."	"I don't want this."	
	"I prefer to do this."	"They do."	
	"I will go along with them this time."	"They made me do it." "I forgot, tried but didn't make it, etc."	
	3		4

(Left axis: Young People's Response to the Influence — Acceptance / Denial; Right axis: Denial)

Outside the Person

Table 1 reflects different ways in which individuals may experience peer influence. The axis from left to right considers from where the individual feels the influence coming. The influence may feel as if it were coming from inside the person or from the outside environment. The axis from top to bottom considers the individual's response to the felt influence. A person can respond with a clear-eyed acceptance of the influence's source or with confused denial. These two axes lead to a four-part picture of how young persons experience peer influence.

Square 1 combines the experience of internal influence with acceptance of those inner desires. Jason wants to begin acting on his own, independent of his parents, but he believes that he is still unready to step away totally. He wants to know himself better and needs the encouragement of friends to try new ways of thinking and behaving. Jason says to himself, "I want what this group offers me. I want their friendship, support, and the chances to do things with them during this time in my life. Acting as a member of this group meets my present needs." Jason feels inclined to go along with the group rules for now and does so deliberately. He chooses to belong because he knows it can help him become more independent of home.

Square 2 combines the influence coming from inside the person with the denial response. These young people feel their internal messages as if they were pressure coming from outside themselves. Their inner wishes seem so disturbing, so contrary to the way their parents, religion, or society taught them to view the world that admitting their innermost desires openly would be too frightening. They believe that if they were to admit these wishes aloud to themselves, they would face a terrible punishment. Susan wants to go shopping with her friends. The girls, all fifteen years old, want the chance to shop, flirt with young men they know will be there, and perhaps set up dates for that night. Susan and her friends do meet several young men, and they all agree to meet again that evening. Susan knows how vigorously her parents would object if they knew what was on her friends' minds. Her folks strongly object to premarital sexual behavior of any kind. Her father might even take his belt to her backside again. Susan wants to join her friends but is so afraid of wanting to be part of their boy-girl activity that the only message she hears seems to be the one coming from outside herself. It is her friends who want to meet guys, not she, she tells herself. "They want to get picked up, not me!" Like the big screen at the movie theater, Susan sees only the projected objects; she forgets that the objects come from the machine clicking quickly in the upstairs booth. She denies that she wants to be picked up, too.

Adolescents who have not learned how to sort through and reflect on their own internal experiences, emotions, and thoughts sometimes deny their own thoughts and wishes in this way. Thinking about one's subjective moods and thoughts is unfamiliar behavior. Young adolescents often lack the emotional maturity and intellectual tools to practice reflective thinking regularly. They do not understand the effective problem-solving process. Many believe life is simply a matter of reacting to whatever happens. This is the way others appear to live their lives. These young people are not aware that a more competent way of responding to life's events exists.

Other young adolescents sometimes discover that beginning to look for the emotion or thought behind the inner tension just produces more tension. They cannot stand the wait until they can find the right internal cue causing the discomfort. Occasionally these young people feel as if they will literally explode from the inner tension. Then they act impulsively at the first opportunity just to get rid of the uncomfortable feeling. Any action feels better than no action at all. They cannot wait until an occasion that might really solve their problem arises. Persons like these frequently experience internal demands as if they were coming from others outside themselves. The defense mechanism called projection allows persons to act without having to say, "I did it and I am responsible." For a time, they fool themselves into believing the prompting to action came from an outside source.

Square 3 links peer influence coming from outside the person with the response of acceptance. The group may expect its members to socialize only with members of other "acceptable" cliques. Brian wants to date a girl from his algebra class. Many of his friends consider her to be "too straight to be interesting." Brian says to himself, "I'd like to know Janet better, but the guys will probably laugh at me if I go out with her. I like the guys a lot. I enjoy their friendship, and I appreciate their support. Janet may be nice, but choosing to date her at this time is not worth the risk of losing the fellows' respect and acceptance.'' Brian chooses to go along with group expectations because doing so meets his present needs.

Square 4 brings together the experience of external peer influence with denial. The peer group influences its members to think and behave in certain ways. Every act of conformity shows the group members that they must be right since so many are acting this way. One member following the rules justifies all, so the group members forcefully press their case. In this situation, the members experience the influence as pressure. Shirley wants to complete her geography essay, which is due Monday, but her friends have decided to meet Sunday afternoon at one member's house for corn chips and conversation. They say that all members *must* attend. Shirley wants to do both things but knows she must choose between them. As much as she wants to have her assignment completed on time, she is not ready at this point to risk angering the group members or losing their friendship. When her mother confronts her two weeks later about the poor grade in geography, Shirley answers, "It was important that I attend the Sunday meeting. The other girls insisted that I do it.'' She excuses away her responsibility with ''They made me do it!''

Choice and responsibility run through each part of this model. Individuals can feel internal influence from unmet needs and goals. Likewise, peer groups can exert strong influence on individuals to think and act in certain ways. Individuals ready to reject group expectations must also be ready to reject the intimacy, acceptance, support, access, approval, and sense of identity the group provides. Persons must, however, decide whether or not to recognize and admit their internal or external forces. If they then decide to act, they must decide how to put their information into action. If one feels slighted by a thoughtless friend, the injured person must first realize what the unpleasant sensation inside is, discover what created it, and decide what to do about it. Should the injured person confront the thoughtless friend about the cruel behavior or decide to drop the whole episode as understandable but unimportant?

A perception, thought, or need gives information about that person's experience. The choice about whether or not to turn the information into action, and if so, how, belongs to that person. If some group members want to go out for pizza after the basketball game, but Sal told his parents he would come home immediately after the final quarter, he has a choice to make. Should he decide to go with his friends or follow through on his agreement with his parents? If he selects the first alternative, he may need to phone home soon and tell his folks about the change in plans so they won't worry. If Sal selects the second option, he may need to explain the original arrangement to his friends and find another way home. Regardless of which decision Sal makes, he is still responsible for his actions and must be ready to answer for them to friends and parents.

In this instance, the individual responds to internal and external influences. He accepts both and makes an aware decision about how he will resolve the situation.

Another person might handle this same situation with a lack of responsibility. Megan's friends ask her to come with them for burritos after the game, but her parents expected her to come home right after the last quarter. Megan feels the internal influence to remain part of the group and have a good time as well as the influence to stick with her original plan to go home. She believes that missing the excitement and fun with her friends is a worse penalty than facing her parents' anger. She would rather have her parents yell at her than feel left out of her friends' activities. Her parents will be angry but will still love her. Her friends might not. Megan thinks, "My friends want me to join them. Nothing else is important to me right now." She avoids thinking about her parents until she is walking up the front steps to her house hours later. When questioned the next morning by her folks, Megan says she forgot to call home about her change in plans. She cries "They made me go along with them." She avoids her own responsibility for choosing an alternative by denying her part in the situation with flimsy excuses.

Areas of Peer Pressure

Peer groups spell out the "correct" ways of thinking and doing for their members. Some peer groups have only a few clear rules. Groups may say which persons can be active members and which nonmembers are "acceptable" but not truly "insiders." Other groups have more or different rules of correctness. Generally, the peer group directs many areas of adolescent life. Not following these rules leaves the disobedient individual open to group disapproval and loss of membership.

Friends   Primarily, the groups decide which persons are "in" and which are "out". Usually groups of adolescent girls place more emphasis than do adolescent boys on who is acceptable for membership and who is not. Studies find teenage girls value qualities of empathy, intimacy, and dependency in their friendships, while their male counterparts stress skills, achievement, and self-sufficiency.[6] These

[6] Douvan, E., and Adelson, J., *The Adolescence Experience* (New York: Wiley, 1966), cited in Coleman, John C., "Friendship and the Peer Group in Adolescence," Joseph Adelson, ed., *Handbook of Adolescent Psychology* (New York: Wiley, 1980).

characteristics reflect the societal values with which these young people are raised. For many girls, becoming members of a local sorority or club is an all-or-nothing matter. Those invited to join may wear special emblem jackets and date the ''best'' young men. An important public show of these young women's worth and acceptability arrives with their membership bids. No wonder those not invited to join suspect their lives are over. In a way, their social life with that particular group ends. For young men, on the other hand, emphasis on activity and independence does not encourage the development of close, intimate relationships among friends.

Clear group identities appear in early adolescence. A group of friends may form around a particular value or activity. Academic peer groups form among people who find each other in advanced school courses. They sit next to one another in Honors English and World History. They set a premium on obtaining high grades and displaying intelligence. They compete with their intellects. Personalities and social backgrounds play less important roles in these groups while the individuals are in school.

Social peer groups form among adolescents who live in the same neighborhood, share similar socioeconomic backgrounds, value having a certain style of wardrobe, and show the right social poise. Their manner reflects their particular experience and self-assurance. The social group of friends from uptown may seem nothing like the social group from downtown only because the details of address, parental paychecks, clothing styles, and habits vary. Social peer groups often strongly define which friends are okay and which are OUT.

Athletic peer groups create another type of friendship group. These young people join to share an interest in playing and competing in sports and in boosting general physical development. The more skill young persons show in sports, the greater value their membership brings to the group. Athletic peer groups often have flexible rules. Friends spend much time together playing sports but remain free to join other peer groups outside the arena.

Individuals may be members of several peer groups at the same time. Bill belongs to an academic group because he earns high grades and participates in a social group because his friends live in the same neighborhood and share similar values and interests. He also stays active in an athletic peer group that appreciates his varsity abilities. Young women have similar chances to belong to several peer groups. Individuals then choose with which friends to spend time. A different activity means seeking out different friends.

Two other friendship groups exist in the schools and communities during adolescence. Group misfits consist of unhappy, lonely adolescents who come together seeking each other's approval and support. Confused, angry young people look for others like themselves. Together they feel as if someone finally understands them. The rules in these groups are often inflexible as the groups fight to present publicly their image of confidence and well-being while most of the members secretly believe that they are neither confident nor acceptable. Many members feel rebellious toward all adult authority, keep personal concerns to themselves, value deliberately dressing in a unfashionable style, and loudly declare's school's unimportance. They prefer adventure and excitement today rather than planning for an uncertain future. This attitude occasionally leads to illegal or unacceptable behaviors. This group, however, often acts first to welcome a lonely or isolated newcomer in the school or neighborhood. They offer friendship to strangers because they understand what it means to feel left out, and they believe they need all the supportive membership they can get.

Finally, some young adolescents remain apart from peer groups. Some individuals have unique or specialized interests that few peers share. Some have a fascination with instrumental music, building electronic generators, or analyzing military history, pursuits best followed alone. In early adolescence, they remain apart from close-knit groups because they focus more toward their special interests than on social activities. Many think themselves unlike most people and lack the social skills needed to gain entry into a friendship group or to develop and keep relationships. With increasing maturity, these young people begin to find other persons with unusual interests or personalities like their own, and they come together in small groups. With ability, talent, motivation, and opportunities, many of these adolescents show a great deal of creativity in their interest areas. They are less likely than other young people to keep their opinions to themselves for fear of what others might think. They often become the least likely adolescents to give in to peer pressure. Moreover, they have confidence in themselves as separate individuals. They feel no need to be like others in every way.

A school or community contains several academic, social, athletic, misfit, and creative groups. Individual group members sometimes find their own group encouraging them to interact with persons from different groups. For instance, one social group respects members able to win friends and opportunities for participation in other groups. The more connections a group member makes, the more the original peer group gains. On the other hand, a peer group may actively discourage its members from making friendly contacts with persons from other groups. In this case, the discouraging peer group members are insecure, anxious persons ready to suspect these exchanges with outsiders as sellouts. Becoming friendly with outsiders means betrayal, possibly threatening the entire group, its values, and its public face. This insecure group puts a heavy pressure on its members to stay true and loyal only to one another.

Secrets   To young people, having secrets signals adulthood. How many times have parents stopped a conversation in mid-sentence when junior entered the room? Having secrets seems like an adult behavior.

Having secrets also guarantees privacy. Separating from parents becomes an important issue during adolescence, and keeping quiet about their thoughts and actions allows young people to live their own lives beyond their parents' awareness. Begging for an extension phone in their bedroom, writing a diary and hiding the key, sending notes to friends, and not discussing with parents every idea or event in which they are involved accomplishes this end.

Peer groups often use the need for secrets as a way to control their members. Rumors and gossip effectively keep straying members in line. Robin met Susan in her psychology class and wanted to know her better. Robin invited Susan to join her and her other friends for a soda after school. Robin and Susan began to develop a serious friendship as they learned that they had much in common. After several lunches and after-school snacks with the group, Robin's friend Margaret took Susan aside and started telling her stories about Robin's supposedly faltering relationship with a current boyfriend. Susan swore secrecy. Meanwhile, Margaret went back to Robin and told her that Susan has been making nasty remarks about Robin's boyfriend behind her back. Margaret also told Robin she had promised Susan she wouldn't say anything to Robin about their talk but had reluctantly decided to tell Robin anyway because they were such dear friends. Robin became furious but said nothing to Susan, whom she now viewed as a disloyal betrayer. Robin stopped spending time outside class with Susan. Soon everyone was confused and hurt except Margaret. She won this episode of guerrilla-warfare-by-gossip. Shifts occurring in friendships among adolescents upset those feeling left out by the new arrangements. In this instance, Margaret brought things back to the way they were in the beginning by shutting Susan out. In addition, she rebuilt her weakened self-esteem at Susan's and Robin's expense.

Rumor and gossip can influence who's in and who's out. They can also support the group against the threat of the unknown by making individuals who are slightly different seem to be very different. Sharon's parents divorced while she was in junior high school, and each remarried several years later. This bright, attractive, and popular girl's world split in two when her mother moved across the country. Sharon moved in with her newly remarried father and his young bride. Too busy with their own work and with each other, Sharon's father and stepmother gave her little time or supervision. From a perky ninth grader, Sharon gradually grew into a lovely young woman in the eleventh grade. Her interest in coursework fell, and she began staying out late at night with friends. Both the social and academic groups of which Sharon was once a vital part started gossiping about her dates, her imagined drinking escapades, and embellished hearsay about her sneaking out of the house at night. Unable to understand the change in her attitude and behavior, the peer groups branded Sharon a Scarlet Woman by age sixteen, and they dropped her from membership. Stories of Sharon's sexuality and sophistication upset them, and they broke their ties to her with put-downs and rumors. Gossiping was easier than trying to understand a confused, unhappy Sharon and more comfortable than trying to accept their own emerging sexuality.

Romance   Peer groups influence the amount of romance in their members' lives. Romance feels like strong, forceful emotions. Adolescents value experiences that produce these novel feelings. It is like nothing they ever felt before. Sentimental love, athletic powers, and adventure satisfy adolescents' romantic leanings. If the peer group openly values boy-girl relationships, many of its members will seek opposite-sex relationships. If the group prizes dreamed-of-but-unobtainable-love, many of its members will always seem to have disturbing problems with boyfriends or girlfriends. If the group applauds scoring points during athletic contests, its members will frequently engage in competition or rehash the last game. In these ways, group members behave in ways that bring them the respect and support of other group members. These actions, in turn, further strengthen the group's image and rules.

Romance can become a private event as well as a public one. Many adolescents daydream or fantasize. These mental plays meet several needs. Fantasies may be escapist as the person seeks to get away from stress in daily life. Daydreaming about meeting the right man prevents an adolescent girl from facing a lonely, unpopular present while she also avoids thinking about ways to improve it. Daydreaming about last weekend's championship wrestling match feels more satisfying than paying attention to an English teacher's lecture right now.

Fantasies may serve as a rehearsal in which future roles are mentally tested and rated. One person may fantasize about asking a certain young lady to go with him to the

movies Friday night. He can safely explore different ways
of phrasing his request, consider the best time to ask her,
and think about what they might do after the show. Another person may mentally practice the whole process of
taking a competitive exam, from sharpening pencils, to
finding a seat, to not knowing an answer, as a way to
overcome test anxiety.

Daydreams review not only pleasant situations but also
troubling ones. Past interactions that somehow went wrong
can be mentally replayed and alternative approaches for
improving the situation found. A girl thinks her track coach
is unfairly pressuring her to remain on the team when she
really wants to quit. She'd rather spend the time on a part-
time job. Yet whenever she is about to mention the subject
of leaving, she and the coach always begin arguing about
something else, and she never speaks of quitting. If the
girl would think over the details of their interactions and
see at which point the real message becomes lost, she could
determine better ways to say what she means.

Reveries of these kinds represent the adolescents' emotional growth. They are learning how to elaborate their
thoughts and feelings. To the outsider, such as a busy parent, a young person sitting on the sofa staring blankly at
the mantel clock looks like a loafer. It may, however, be
an important time for maturation of intellect and behavior.

Clothes   Wardrobe is another important area of adolescence subject to peer pressure. From shoe styles to hair
styles and everything in between, adolescents communicate with their clothes.

A person's style of dressing tells much about that individual's group status. Like an identification badge, one's
wardrobe tells to which peer group one belongs. One group
will dress "up" in skirts, sweaters, pressed shirts, and re-

spectable leather shoes while another group dresses "down" with unwashed, unpressed jeans, pullovers, and well-worn sneakers. Obtaining the right color, the right manufacturer's label, the right "look" becomes all-important in gaining peer approval.

Among some peer groups, wardrobe ranks higher than school grades, extracurricular achievements, or social skills. One chic young man who arrived well-dressed to the last detail at school every morning for two weeks never attended a single class. Status-by-wardrobe is easier to attain than are many of the traditional ways to earn respect. All one needs is a fashion eye and lots of money. A fine wardrobe, however, is not merely the territory of well-to-do children from prosperous neighborhoods. Many adolescents from poor families dress in a manner out of all proportion to their families' incomes.

For peer groups, clothing also tells about gender. Physical sex differences between boys and girls become more noticeable at puberty. Many young adolescents are uncomfortably self-conscious about their changing bodies. Some peer groups stress the unisex look of jeans or overalls, loose shirts, and athletic shoes for all members. The individuals can then mask their gender with both males and females wearing identical styles. Other peer groups that view physical maturity as an important symbol of adulthood encourage members to dress in ways that highlight their male or female characteristics. Revealingly tight slacks, low-buttoned shirts for boys, sheer blouses and side-slit skirts for girls play up their blossoming sexuality.

Another message communicated by adolescents' clothing: We are not like our parents! Young people attempt to separate emotionally from their parents as a way to begin self-direction and responsibility. Wearing outfits that differ sharply from their parents' attire becomes an outward sign of this inward separateness. Each peer group establishes the details of this differentness. Whether it is sloppy, casual, flashy, or preppy, members' dress conforms to the peer code as styles distinct from those of adults in their lives.

Finally, teenagers' wardrobes may be a vehicle for personal expression. Young people dress in ways reflecting their moods, self-images, or needs of the moment. The person will decide what is appropriate, when, where, and how. Color, style, and purpose become matters for flexible personal choice. The freedom to dress for self-expression comes in later adolescence when individuals better understand themselves and have more confidence in standing apart from the group. By this time in their lives, they can even gain new respect and admiration for the novel and exciting ways in which they coordinate their wardrobes.

Telephone Use   Parents and siblings frequently swing between amusement and resentment at adolescents' telephone behavior. At all hours and for all reasons, teenagers seem dependent on the telephone as if it were a lifeline. Over the phone, adolescents discuss daily events, swap gossip, solve chemistry homework problems, decide what to wear for the next party, complain about teachers and parents, and build more intimate relationships with their friends.

Dialing out and receiving phone calls at home marks adolescents as adults. Connecting by telephone with other individuals certifies to these young people that they have important lives beyond their families. Their reliance on parents for advice and support seems to grow less with each exchange over the phone.

In addition, telephone involvement becomes a major way

in which young people can check out their perceptions of the world. If their view meshes with their friends' views, when both parties can agree on what they say and what it means, both can validate reality. In this way, their confidence in assessing real-world situations and making the correct decisions increases. When the two views are not the same, and one friend judges a situation differently from the other, young people gain a more realistic view of themselves and the important events in their lives.

Drug Use   Adolescents experiment with marijuana and alcohol. They want to see for themselves what the uproar is all about. Drugs meet many needs of young people seeking to understand themselves better and find their place in the world.

Young people are curious and adventurous. Using drugs gives a chance to meet both needs. To many, drug use becomes a symbol of adulthood. Since adults use prescription medications, and movies and magazines show adults using drugs or alcoholic beverages for recreation, these illegal or "sophisticated" items attract individuals wanting to appear grown-up. Since parents fuss and fume about their evils, adolescents view drugs and their use as ways to assert their independence from parental control. Here are behaviors they can do when their parents aren't looking or able to stop them. Drug use can be a key behavior needed to become a member of a certain peer group. The rebellious and often taboo acts help mark the group's identity and note which persons are acceptable members. To others, drug use offers a "time out" from the difficult pressures and unanswerable questions of who am I, where am I going, and how am I going to get there?

Although drug use among adolescents appears to be declining since the late 1970's,[7] many young people do experiment with drugs. They take an occasional toke or drink beer to see how the drugs affect them and their relationships. The majority of teens—53 percent of thirteen- to fifteen-year-olds and 78 percent of sixteen- to eighteen-year-olds—say they drink alcohol occasionally. Almost 75 percent of high schoolers say they have tried marijuana.[8] They try drugs once or use them for awhile. They satisfy their curiosity, then stop.

Approximately 9 percent of adolescents become drug abusers.[9] They continue to smoke marijuana or drink alcoholic beverages regularly because the rebellious act and the drugs' effect are important to them. They value the peer approval they receive for these acts. They value the temporary relief from the difficult tasks they face as they become older. Abuse begins when all their energies become focused on obtaining or using drugs rather than on learning the necessary attitudes and skills essential for survival in this challenging, complex society.

Drug abusers share many characteristics. They think poorly of themselves and their own worth. They deeply fear that they are not good enough, smart enough, attractive enough, talented enough, or popular enough to be successful in a threatening, unpredictable world. The abusers also have high expectations for what they want to achieve. Their ambitious goals—to have friends, to earn strong grades in school, to excel in some activity they see as important, to build a satisfying and successful career—clash sharply with their low opinion of themselves and their abilities to make their wishes come true. Wanting so much,

[7] Sullivan, Ronald, "Teens Share Growing Concern Over Drugs' Effects," Newport News *Daily Press,* July 20, 1981, p. 5.

[8] "160,000 Teenagers Talk About Their Lives," *McCall's* (October 1981), p. 46.

[9] "Drug Use Declining Among Teens: Expert," Newport News *Daily Press* (July 28, 1981), p. 2.

yet expecting so little to happen, these discouraged adolescents fear greater disappointments ahead.

In addition, these young abusers have trouble waiting. When they feel an impulse to act, they act, often without thinking about the consequences. If the outcome is unpleasant, they quickly and blindly act again to change the situation. They dig themselves a hole and when they don't like the view, they just keep on digging deeper. These young people feel great inner tensions and act mainly to get rid of those unpleasant feelings. They lack the confidence in their ability to wait, think, plan, and then gradually change the situations in ways that might truly please them in the long run. Likewise, these young people are fearful and guilty about their own thoughts and feelings. Tracing thoughts and feelings back to their meaning makes them nervous. They use drugs to erase these disturbing elements for the time being.

Drug-abusing adolescents' lack of self-confidence means they avoid the very opportunities to develop skills that might build the confidence necessary to move toward mature adulthood. They don't work hard in their classes, and they miss building the intellectual skills they need to solve problems and move toward a vocation. They avoid new arenas for physical challenges—skating, karate, ballet, team sports—that would build physical stamina, grace, and skills to give them confidence in their bodies. They avoid entering new social situations—parties, dances, clubs—that would help them develop poise and skills in meeting and liking other people. Feeling bad about themselves, drug-abusing adolescents stay away from the situations that might really help them the most. Instead, they trap themselves in a cycle of drugs and irresponsibility, falling further and further behind their age-mates in developing adult survival skills.

Driving To adolescents, driving represents freedom, independence, power, and maturity. This activity requires adult abilities, skills, and sound judgment to do well. It also requires a young person to reach a certain age before being legally permitted to get a license. Driving a car is a vivid symbol of adulthood.

Cars provide an especially important symbol to young men. Adolescent males highly prize their automobiles and take pride in understanding their inner workings. Cars represent more than a way to get from here to there. They become "other selves," tinkered with and finely tuned machines that present a young man's public face to the world. Slick shine or rattletrap: love me, love my car.

Carrying such importance to adolescents, driving often becomes a pawn of peer pressure. Friends goad each other into looking "macho" by behaving in adventurous, foolhardy ways behind the wheel. They sit too many people inside the car, creating distracting noise and disturbing the driver. They mix drinking or other drugs with driving, dulling the driver's senses and slowing response times. They encourage the driver to travel too fast for the road or weather conditions. Tragedy often results. Auto accidents are the main cause of death during the adolescence years.

On the other hand, car use can be a way to teach young people about responsibility. Learning to attend to weather, road conditions, the car's responsiveness, passenger safety, and one's own alertness contributes to becoming an effective driver and a considerate adult. Driving a car successfully teaches young people to anticipate and solve problems as they develop. Sharing a car with family members increases appreciation for others and encourages sensitivity to their needs.

For young people, cars can be a positive learning experience or a dangerous weapon. Adolescents who act impulsively, who lash out when angry, or who act in untrustworthy ways suggesting poor judgment and little willingness to plan ahead, make bad drivers. An auto may be an instrument for peer pressure or a vehicle with which to build true maturity.

Attitude Toward Growth and Change   Peer groups often influence subtle areas of behavior. The within-the-individual behaviors of self-awareness and reflective thinking come under peer influence. Some peer groups value these characteristics. They encourage self-awareness activities in their members by giving opportunities for individuals to discuss intimate or troubling concerns. Other members respond to this openness with increased support, caring, and possible alternative solutions for the troubled person. For such groups, only shallow people do not look inward in a thoughtful way. Similar groups might encourage individuals to think back while alone and then report their insights or conclusions to the group. Members are free to respond to new situations in the most effective manner for that person under those circumstances. Growth and change in the members is okay and does not threaten the group's well-being.

On the other hand, some peer groups actively discourage this type of intrapersonal behavior. These behaviors feel uncomfortable inside and arouse an inner tension for the individuals experiencing them. To begin identifying a feeling or thought starts a physiological excitement that at first seems overwhelming. Ginny, age fifteen, drank alcohol daily for the specific purpose of numbing her thought processes. She cried that trying to understand herself was so terrifying that her body trembled at the idea. Alcohol cut the process short, helping her feel in control again. Ginny and her friends drank before school, at lunch, and on the way home. For this group, only "squares" or "holier-than-thou's" did not drink regularly. To look at one's feelings was silly and sentimental. This attitude and behavior works against young people's meeting new situations in flexible and constructive ways. Personal growth and change in this group represent a severe threat because members feel terror enough at trying to master the present. Change just ups the stakes.

Whether or not a peer group encourages development of self-awareness and responsible decision-making depends upon the group's collective feelings about themselves. A group in which most members experience positive feelings and views about themselves can put up with the very real tension of tracing uncomfortable emotions and thoughts to their source. They know that they are strong enough to withstand any internal pressures without falling apart. Moreover, they trust themselves and each other to provide necessary support in times of difficulty. For groups consisting mainly of persons who do not like or trust themselves, thoughts that they suspect might start feelings of guilt or anxiety or raise unanswerable questions are to be strictly avoided. Since they cannot trust themselves, they cannot trust one another to be there for them when most needed.

Peer Counselors

While peer pressure can influence young people to experiment with or abuse drugs and alcohol, so can peer pressure work in positive ways to prevent the use of these substances.

Young people often seek each other when they want to talk about important things. They value their friends' advice and want to act in ways that please their friends.

Peer counselors, sometimes called peer partners, peer helpers, natural helpers, or peer facilitators, are groups of young people trained in effective listening and helping skills who work with teens in schools and communities to help them make better decisions and solve problems. These peer counselors usually are from a variety of backgrounds and neighborhoods. Here are good students and so-so students. Here are athletes and others who can't tell a baseball from a volleyball. Peer counselors are students with closets full of clothes and students with two flannel shirts and one just-washed pair of jeans. They are from uptown, downtown, and midtown. What they share is the same school and the desire to help other persons make better choices and learn to solve their problems and live happier lives.

Adult trainers teach these young people helping skills. Teens learn to be good listeners. They learn to become sensitive to body language and subtle comments of concern that others overlook. Peer counselors learn to paraphrase and summarize what others are saying. They learn to listen for the emotional meaning behind the words and to ask the speaker to say more about what really matters to him or her.

Peer counselors also learn the steps to good problem-solving and decision-making. They learn to help others say just what is the problem. They ask what the individual wants to be the result. They help the person look at the choices for action to reach that end and weigh the good and bad parts of each alternative. They help the person decide which plan of action he or she wants to take and when to do it. Then peer counselors work with the person to review the action, see what happened, and judge whether the desired result was achieved.

Trained peer counselors really hear what their classmates are saying. They hear about how negative peer pressure hurts their classmates. They hear of young people who fear that their friends won't like them if they don't drink beer at parties, if they don't smoke grass when a joint is passed around, or if they don't go to bed with their boyfriend or girlfriend. Peer counselors hear stories about bad relationships with friends and parents. They hear sad tales of classmates who feel so helpless and hopeless that they are thinking of killing themselves. They hear of young people not knowing what to do and not wanting to hurt others or themselves by making the wrong choice. For some, just talking aloud about problems makes them feel better. To have someone else really understand what they mean makes them feel better.

"Just Say No"

The "Just Say No" program uses positive peer pressure to influence young people to live drug-free lives. Elementary school and junior high students join together in classroom groups or in clubs led by adult sponsors to learn more about drugs and the dangers they cause and to plan activities to make classmates aware of those dangers. They make posters and banners and stage skits to bring their positive message to others. They take the "Just Say No" pledge and sing "Just Say No" songs. Every year youth from schools across the country sponsor a "Just Say No" week and day. They act in unison with marches, walks, and balloon launches, and thousands of voices are heard as one voice with others sharing the same antidrug beliefs. With these activities continued over time, positive peer pressure works to keep youngsters from looking to drugs or alcohol as either recreation or escape.

In a similar way, many states are looking to their youth

as leaders in the fight against drug and alcohol use among teens. Virginia, for example, started a Youth Alcohol Abuse Prevention Project (YAAPP) in 1985 to train student leaders to develop school-based programs for the prevention of alcohol and drug abuse. Their goals were to reduce the use of alcohol and drugs among high school students and to lower the rate of alcohol-related accidents among teens. The project informed student leaders about drugs and safety and taught specific skills for starting drug-free programs such as Students Against Drunk Driving (SADD) or Operation Prom/Graduation. Not only was there a 29 percent increase in school-based, teen-sponsored and -led prevention activities for students in 1985–86, but Department of Motor Vehicle statistics showed a drop from 48 to 37 percent in the number of student drivers involved in fatal, alcohol-related accidents from 1984 to 1985[10]. Through positive peer pressure, Virginia high school students are sending their classmates the message that drinking, drug abuse, and driving kill other teens.

Conclusion

Peer pressure is an important influence on young people's attitudes and behaviors. Groups of similar young people offer independence from the family, acceptance, a sense of personal worth, support in times of confusion, guides for appropriate conduct in a complex world, and social identity. Many factors affect how peer influence feels and how the individual will respond to its force. At one time or another, most adolescents choose to go along

[10]Coleman, M.M. (1986). "Alcohol, drug abuse: Teens fight back," *Public Education, A magazine of the Virginia Department of Education*, 22(3), Fall, 1986, 8.

with group expectations in exchange for having their needs met. In addition, peer influence enters many areas of adolescent lives, public and private. Peer pressure makes a large impact on important attitudes and behaviors that can encourage or deter adolescents' maturity of judgment and action.

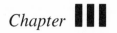

Peer Pressure, Achievement, and Adventure

Adolescents want to become independent of their parents. They want to be able to make intelligent decisions about their own lives and to live with satisfying outcomes. To do this, young people gradually build a collection of attitudes and skills gained through their interactions with their environment and with other people. They need skills in self-understanding and effective decision-making, skills in developing and maintaining relationships, and skills in performing the vocational tasks by which they will eventually earn a livelihood. Adolescents' identities include all of these, and the process of mastering these tasks is the process of self-definition.

Our society provides opportunities for young people to learn these attitudes and abilities. In the past, young people learned them mainly through the family and the church. Adolescents today find many occasions for developing attitudes and skills through classwork, social activities, and extracurricular events. Succeeding in these areas brings self-esteem and the respect of others as well as the crucial abilities needed to become responsible adults. Not succeeding brings chances to face their limitations, build new skills, pick new challenges, or leave the field altogether.

Adventure, too, plays a vital role in adolescent life. Frequently adventure means constructive, wholesome entertainment and recreation. It also means methods to avoid achieving in appropriate and necessary ways.

Adventure and successful achievement both meet many emotional needs during adolescence: chances to prove mettle, win self-esteem and the good opinion of others, and develop essential abilities. Adventure may, on the other hand, provide a means to short-circuit the growth of important attitudes and skills necessary for responsible adulthood.

Adolescent Need for Achievement

As young people mature, they see the world full of exciting possibilities. So many things to observe, experience, and accomplish exist. Any activity, from gardening, to writing an English essay, to becoming a loyal friend, provides an opportunity for more fully understanding the environment as well as for more deeply understanding oneself. The doing and accomplishing in themselves become ways of proving one's worth. "I was here!" "I did this!" Particularly during adolescence when young people work at defining themselves and charting a future direction, achieving and accomplishing are vital processes.

Because the achievement need is learned,[1] the direction that the individual's striving for success takes varies widely from person to person. All persons' achievements reflect their unique past experiences. When parents teach children to value competition, to perform well on different tasks by themselves, and when they give praise for achieving these goals, children learn to look for other chances to perform well and earn more rewards. When Johnny receives his parents' warm smiles and enthusiastic applause for playing

---

[1] Byrne, Donn, *An Introduction to Personality. Research, Theory, and Applications,* 2d ed. (Englewood Cliffs: Prentice-Hall, 1972).

sports successfully, he will likely look for more opportunities to shine on the athletic field. Attention and approval feel good and help build his confidence in this activity. Likewise for Matt and his reading, or Jenny and her drawing. Children do more of what they receive praise or glowing attention for doing.

Alternately, if parents equally accept success or failure, their children do not necessarily see their own accomplishments as ways to gain parental approval or increase self-esteem. Building a need for achievement is not a one-time event. It is an ongoing process of give and take between the individuals and those who influence their behavior by saying, "Do it well" and "Do it on your own."

Adolescence represents a special time for achievement. Achieving now becomes a way adolescents define themselves and gain approval from peers and adults. Seeking independence from parents, the young people want to "do it well." Adultlike attitudes and behavior are complicated, unclear, and difficult to attain. The peer group provides ways to make achievement more likely. The group spells out how, when, and where to achieve while at the same time helping adolescents to feel accepted and belonging.

Peer Influences on Direction and Amount of Achievement   The peer group influences the direction and amount of adolescent achievement. For young adolescents, achieving and belonging go together. Stepping out in the world apart from parents is an achievement. Deciding for themselves about friends, clothes, spending money, and social behavior are also important achievements. Belonging to a peer group is another achievement. Peer group membership brings agreed upon guidelines for proper thought and action as well as the rewards of respect and approval for performing these well. Gradually, adolescents become more effective as they get involved with the events and people in their lives. These achievements build good feelings and new skills; adolescents gain confidence in their abilities to master life situations. Successful achievements strengthen their good images of themselves and build assurance in their own opinions and solutions. Eventually, as they become older and more experienced, they will be able to move beyond the group's consensus about what is correct and take truly independent thought and action.

Meanwhile, the peer group in early and middle adolescence greatly influences the direction and amount of adolescent achievement. Peer influence occurs in academic areas. Intellectually talented students in accelerated academic classes together frequently compete with imagination, productivity, and excellent grades. Contributing novel ideas to class discussions, showing off-handed humor about the subject at hand that only ''insiders'' can appreciate, and earning top grades from demanding teachers are all ways in which this group achieves and receives rewards. Academic groups often encourage open competition with comparisons of report cards and standardized test scores. Other bright groups may prefer a more quiet, low-key approach to high performance and choose to remain smugly silent about their success until asked. In these academic groups, peer pressure contributes to building educational skills and constructive work.

A different peer group encourages its members to achieve in social areas. When the important group members begin dating and gain their friends' approval by becoming part of a couple, other members start feeling pressure to begin dating. Another group values filling the leadership roles in school, so the members expect to run for class offices or seek the yearbook editorship. Still another peer group finds importance through sexual behavior and encourages its members' sexual activities. Their talk often revolves around boy-girl relationships, who's ''doing it'' and who's not. Their actions attempt to imitate adults' sophisticated sexuality. Members wear sensual or revealing clothing, flirt, and have a lot of male-female contact through talk and touch.

Yet another adolescent group stresses achievement through wardrobe and parties. All the group members dress smartly in the latest style. They are either in the middle of planning their next get-together or reviewing the details of their last one. Groups that emphasize social achievements help members develop many interpersonal skills by providing opportunities to practice and refine these attitudes and behaviors within the group setting.

Other peer groups value vocational achievement. They spend time discussing the pro's and con's of various colleges or careers or the wisdom of joining the military services. One group encourages its members to take part-time jobs after school, enabling them to assume some adult responsibility, appear mature and competent, and have spending money to use as they please. When members meet as a group, they sometimes talk about their supervisors or co-workers, recount exciting happenings at work, or grumble about on-the-job annoyances. The achievement direction in these groups helps members develop appropriate work attitudes, skills, and habits to use throughout their adult lives.

Peer groups approve one or several paths for acceptable achievement. Some adolescents' groups value academic, interpersonal, and leadership achievements. Groups may reward social and vocational achievements. Several groups of high performers frequently find their members earning high grades in honors classes, holding offices in the most respected school organizations, and being fashion-conscious individuals enjoying occasional parties and dates in addition to working on after-school, weekend, or summer jobs. Exhausting unless well organized, this schedule permits skill growth in many areas while the adolescents achieve increasing mastery of their environments and build confidence in their abilities to handle present and upcoming events.

When Adolescents Fail   On the other hand, some peer groups reject these established ways of achieving. Atkinson[2], a pioneer in the study of achievement motivation, proposed that people achieve when they get pleasure from striving and accomplishing something. They work hard when they expect their efforts will pay off in a satisfying way. An attractive goal gives additional reason to act. Nat gladly spent hours preparing to write his English term paper: reading books, taking notes, and scribbling tentative outlines on yellow pads. His past experience writing essays told him that this approach paid off in smooth writing now and high grades on the assignments later. Nat expected the preparation activities would help in the long run. The better understanding of his topic and his teacher's respect for his thoroughness offered the incentives. He expected to succeed; he hadn't yet earned less than a B on any major paper.

For Diane, though, the situation differed. She enjoyed English class in middle school because grammar study seemed fun and predictable, and she liked the characters in her literature books. In eighth grade she earned B's, but her ninth-grade teacher expected fewer grammar exercises, more in-depth literary analysis, and a higher quality of written expression. Diane began bringing home C's and

---

[2] Atkinson, John W., "Motivational Determinants of Risk-taking Behavior," *Psychological Review 64* (1957): 359–372.

D's. The teacher offered constructive comments in the margins, but Diane saw these notes as put-downs and avoided reading them. Her confidence in English class fell. Soon she could not write her World History essays or her science papers. No idea seemed good enough. Her sentences seemed to lead nowhere. To her, every word looked trite. While the incentives remained high—Diane wanted high grades and her teachers' respect—she had such low expectation for success that she froze. She didn't know whether to try harder or to throw up her hands in disgust. Diane could do nothing, and her papers continued to decline in quality or be left incomplete on her desk.

Several factors contribute to adolescents' achievement. Young people must want the rewards offered for successful outcomes. They must have the confidence in their own ability to meet the challenge. They must be interested in the activity and have the opportunity to get involved. Given these factors, they will usually want to achieve. At times, however, adolescents find achievement blocked. Some young people desire the rewards but lack the specific interest needed to become involved in the activity. Others lack the specific skills needed to perform the task, or miss the opportunity to act. Doris wanted to become a reporter for the school newspaper. She wanted the esteem and recognition of a by-line as well as the chance to list this important activity on her résumé for college. But Doris did not enjoy writing. She earned C's in English class. In addition, Doris had a fast-food job after school that limited her free time. She decided not to try out for the position.

Other causes block achievement. In order to achieve at a high level, adolescents need the attitude that allows them to spend their energies now in order to receive the rewards at some point in the future. James, too, considered joining the school newspaper staff. New to the school, he wanted to build his reputation as a leader and saw this activity as a means to do it. James wrote well, and his papers frequently said interesting things. James understood the four-week span between writing the stories and handing out the finished paper to the student body, but he resented the delay. He decided instead to become a Yell-Leader and get more immediate and widespread visibility by cheering at football games. If James went after the reporter position, it would be to fill other needs than to make himself well known to his classmates.

Most important, adolescents need self-confidence to believe they can focus their energies and abilities on the task at hand. They cannot achieve if they believe they cannot. Young people may have the incentive, the interest, the specific skills as measured by any objective standard, the ability to delay gratification, and the opportunity to perform. If they lack belief in themselves, however, they often pass up the chance to achieve. Dave was a quiet, likable person who scored high enough on standardized tests to be placed in an accelerated eleventh-grade history class. The class had fast-paced and incisive discussions. Although Dave enjoyed reading history books at his leisure, he felt overwhelmed by this verbally aggressive class. He completed his short-answer assignments and test questions but seemed to blank out at the longer essay topics. Dave pushed himself hard to give answers as quick and bright as the others appeared to do easily, but he choked. He began to believe he was dumb and felt too embarrassed to hand in what he suspected to be inferior work. Soon Dave began turning in no work at all and risked failing the course. When he discussed the historical issues with his teacher, one-to-one during a free period, Dave discovered that he could put his thoughts together slowly yet clearly. At times without pressure, he could analyze, interpret, and draw relevant conclusions. Compared to his classmates, however, Dave thought he was a failure. To his mind, the low report card grades publicly confirmed his stupidity. Dave failed not because he was unable or uninterested; he did not lack the opportunity or the desire for the end rewards. Dave failed by default because he thought he would.

How Adolescents Avoid Failing   No one wants to fail. Failing means losing face and losing a sense of personal worth. When individuals' desire to avoid failure becomes stronger than their desire to achieve, they will stay away from situations in which they might have to perform and possibly fall short. Many adolescents join equally discouraged peers in groups where at least they can achieve each other's support and approval. Moreover, many adolescents develop strategies to help cope with their desire to achieve without being overwhelmed by their anticipation of failure.[3]

One strategy helps individuals cope with their fear of failure by picking unrealistic goals. They pick goals so high that no one can blame them for failing or so low that success is a sure thing.

Nelson, a sixteen-year-old who had never been a star in any of his classrooms, said he wanted to become an architect. Nelson took slow-average courses and refused advice to study mechanical drawing or math beyond general arithmetic. He insisted that he wanted to design buildings, and he produced pages of notebook paper filled with partial sketches. He impressed his parents and friends with his lofty goals and his endless drawings. They boasted to others about his bright future. Nelson guaranteed that he would fail, but his unrealistic goal rather than his efforts caused the failure. He did not feel humiliation from missing this

[3] Beery, Richard G., "Fear of Failure in the Student Experience," *Personnel and Guidance Journal 54* (December, 1975) (4): 191–203.

goal. He did not experience failure. Only a miracle or incredible good fortune could have moved Nelson from the actual present to his architecture dream because he lacked the skills to get there and vigorously refused to obtain them. In a variation of this strategy, individuals pick an unrealistically low level of aspiration. Some adolescents avoid failure by under-shooting. They select extremely easy courses or vocational directions well below their abilities. Alice was an award winner many times over for her innovative science projects. She competed on local, state, and national levels throughout her high school years. She wanted eventually to earn a doctorate in astrophysics, and she studied college catalogues trying to determine where to apply for undergraduate study. While waiting to hear from the colleges, Alice flew to a current national science competition. She began enthusiastically, but she returned home three days later rather subdued. She won an Honorable Mention in her category, but the depth and quality of many of the other competitors' projects awed and shook her. Several months later, Alice received offers of full scholarships to three prestigious universities. Alice chose, instead, to attend the smaller technical university in her own state. To Alice, not being ''Number 1'' meant failing. Choosing the less competitive institution meant avoiding the possibility of failing.

Looking at this situation in another way, Alice might have decided to attend the well-known institution and later have dropped out, thereby avoiding the risk of failure. She might have chosen not to attend college at all, saying that she preferred to take a job in her field at a very basic entry level to see if this were truly the right field for her. These alternate strategies would also have helped Alice avoid the risk of failure.

Selecting realistic goals but reducing or blocking investment in them is another strategy to avoid failure. Angela was a high-powered young woman taking advanced courses and participating actively in student government. She had brains, talent, looks, and personality, but when the teachers returned major projects, Angela complained. Her excuses seemed endless. This time, she studied either too little or too late. Her mother kept interrupting her study time with errands for her to do right then. Her favorite movie was on TV, and she couldn't resist. She read part of the material assigned and hoped the rest wouldn't be covered on the test. She really needed a high grade so much that the pressure made her nervous, and she forgot the answers. Once her back began aching during a test, and Angela tearfully asked the teacher if she could visit the school nurse. Because Angela put very little energy into actual studying, she could more easily excuse away the resulting failure than if she had really knocked herself out studying and then failed. Angela could continue to see herself as able and worthwhile. To her, the circumstances led to the failure, not she. Therefore, it did not feel like failure to her.

On the flip-side of this strategy, individuals select realistic goals and find a means to guarantee success. Kirk was bright, able, and a cheat. Crib sheets, copying, talking with friends who had taken the test earlier in the day all contributed to his high grade point standing. He ensured success with these practices. Karen, his classmate, had realistic goals but literally knocked herself out working to get them. Homework, extra reading, getting a head start on major projects, and being a starter on the girls' track team and editor of the school magazine meant that she couldn't turn out the lights before 2 A.M. Her parents objected to her post-midnight routine, but Karen cried that all her friends worked just as hard. If she loosened up, she would lose ground. Four months later, Karen was hospitalized with infectious mononucleosis for two weeks and did not return to school for another three weeks. Her superstriving guaranteed her success until it sidelined her with illness and exhaustion.

How Group Members Avoid Failing   Group members occasionally choose these strategies to avoid failure. Members encourage one another to aim too high and not challenge the goal's unreality. Confronting another with the wishful thinking aspects behind the goal means that the other person might turn and challenge your goals. Sam and his friends sometimes discussed their fantasies about becoming big-name professional athletes. High school stars, they wanted to believe they could win even more applause in the larger world. They used these ambitions as excuses to neglect their schoolwork. It was easier for Sam to pick the easy course, or not put the necessary effort into the harder ones, when his whole circle of friends kept reminding him of his glorious future. Putting off studying was easier when all his friends had the same approach to test-taking. Sam more easily excused a failing grade when his friends said, ''It's not your fault. The teacher just asked nit-picky questions. Besides, we needed you at the basketball game last night.'' It was easier for Sam not to try and to aim low when his friends reassured him, ''The grades aren't worth all the effort. They only prove how long you can stare at a book. What will an A in Algebra mean, anyway, when you're on the court with the Lakers?''

When young people want the rewards but do not expect a positive end, they seek to avoid failure. Through a variety of approaches they choose not to compete. To them, failing means losing self-respect, a sense of personal worth, and the respect of others. At times the group makes avoiding failure easier by using various maneuvers to escape experiencing defeat.

Adolescents also use these strategies to avoid letting their friends down. Sylvie belonged to a group that encouraged high academic performance, but she felt she could not meet her friends' standards. Sylvie's strategy of reduced investment in the goal led her to study too little, too late, and inefficiently. Now and then she "forgot" to bring her books home altogether. Sylvie pointed to her low scores and excused herself with, "I was so busy with my other activities that I didn't have time to study properly."

Alan's group stressed athletic achievement, but he believed he lacked the talent and stamina to star during the season. Alan's plan assured success by trying too hard. During a preseason scrimmage, he threw himself into blocking his opponents, separated his shoulder, and remained sidelined with injuries the rest of the season. His pals called Alan a hero without his ever having to play a regular game.

Michele's friends believed group members should have steady boyfriends and appear at school functions as couples. Michele believed she was not ready for a serious relationship with a young man, so she resisted her peers' pressure with a different plan. She told her friends that she had special feelings for a boy she had met last summer on vacation. He now attended college out of state, and he was unavailable to attend her social events. In this way, Michele saved face but still lived up to group standards. Adolescents employ any number of these approaches in order to avoid failing in their own or in their friends' eyes.

The Lure of Adventure

Adolescents, like most people, value adventure for many reasons. Adventure through relationships or sports represents a romantic activity full of stimulating emotions that fill them with a sense of life's richness. In adventure, young people experience their aliveness in the sharpest way possible. Whether an intense relationship, a leadership role, or mountain climbing, strong emotions and exciting situations result.

Adventure offers a novel change of pace to life's routine. A group of young college men completed their semester and bundled off on a hiking expedition to a nearby national park. These young men were social and academic leaders in their school. The chance to explore and test themselves outdoors, instead of in the library, helped them complete their final exams and set out for the mountains. Zack, the group's organizer, selected the route. He had successfully covered this territory many times before. He picked a path of beautiful open vistas and several difficult turns that would demand serious concentration and effort to travel successfully. Zack and his friends trusted their abilities and efforts on this difficult task. The excitement and pleasure they felt during and after the climb were emotional highs unlike any they had ever known. They could take pride in themselves as physical beings and not just academic grinds. Moreover, adventure represents a means of achieving a good feeling about oneself and the respect of others. Learning to sky-dive, sail a boat, drive a car, or become involved in an exciting relationship requires learning new skills and attitudes in order to complete the attractive activity safely. Sixteen-year-old Fred volunteered to work as an orderly in the hospital emergency room after school so he might experience the life-and-death situations taking place there. He wanted to learn how to help others and how to deal constructively with such crises in his own life. He felt great empathy for the families touched by tragedy, and he admired the doctors' skill and dedication. After several months, Fred had learned enough of the emergency room procedures to assist the doctors in their tasks. They even assigned him certain responsibilities for assisting injured patients and their families. Fred's interest, skill, and personality won the doctors' and nurses' respect and the families' gratitude. Fred loved the work, felt proud of his growing expertise in E. R. techniques, and thrilled to the constant excitement.

The Role of Luck   On their way to becoming independent adults, adolescents want to build a sense of mastery over their world. They want the self-esteem, skills, and confidence that come from succeeding at whatever venture they try. Academic, social, athletic opportunities appear, and young people seek to understand and conquer them.

Not all young people, however, can win the rewards offered for successful achievement in these tasks. Many save face by using strategies that help them avoid the experience of failure. Others accept the limitations of interest, opportunity, ability, or attitude that prevent their success in these activities. Still others think successful achievement depends on luck, and they set out in a different direction. They will achieve through adventure.

A theoretical model exists that describes a way people view their own or others' behavior. In Attribution Theory,[4] individuals identify the outcome of successful or unsuccessful behavior as a result of four factors: the difficulty of the task, luck, effort, and ability. Any or all of these four factors affect the result. For instance, if John won the Student Council election for president, it must have been because his opponent was a real "loser" (easy task), John's friends counted the ballots (luck), John put up many pos-

[4] Weiner, Bernard, and Kukla, Andy, "An Attributional Analysis of Achievement Motivation," *Journal of Personality and Social Psychology 15* (1) (1970): 1–20.

ters and plastered his name all over the halls (effort), or John gave a rousing and popular speech in the nominating assembly and he had lots of leadership experience (ability).

Adolescents frequently use this way of viewing win/lose situations. If they score low on a test, the questions must have been too confusing or unimportant (difficult task), they studied the wrong material (bad luck), or they didn't have enough time to do a respectable job preparing for it (low effort). All these responses save face because they say, "It isn't me; the outside situation led to this poor showing." Many young people think their ability and skills mean the same thing as their personal worth. Low ability equals low worth. To say they failed because they weren't "able" is saying they are unworthy and pitiful. To them, evaluation threatens the loss of everything.

Most achievement situations in adolescence focus on the school and its academic-social-athletic opportunities for striving and excellence. If the young people cannot earn success in these officially approved areas, they will seek success outside them. If low performance brings their abilities and effort into question, they will find other tasks requiring different proportions of task difficulty, ability, effort, and luck. Perhaps the task difficulty or luck—both outside factors—will change.

At these times, adventure represents an alternative to acceptable achievement paths. Adolescents who believe they are not able to succeed in school work, athletics, or popularity often look elsewhere for chances to come out on top. If successful outcomes depend on task difficulty, ability, effort, and luck, and these discouraged young people believe they lack the ability to achieve whatever they want, they can alter the equation to stress task difficulty and luck rather than ability and effort. If the task, such as motorcycle racing, sky-diving, or cutting a record and having a big hit while playing drums with a local band, is difficult enough, no one can blame them for failing and people can only applaud if they win. This brings the fear-of-failure strategy into play again. Likewise, if the task involves enough risk, such as winning a chance to cut a record, using illegal drugs and not getting caught by parents or police, or speeding in the family car while slightly drunk, no one can blame them for failing, either. Through adventure depending on difficult tasks and luck rather than personal skill or effort, adolescents strive for self-respect and the respect of others without the disciplined effort of working toward increasing mastery. Win or lose, adolescent involvement in this type of adventure reduces their experience of failure.

Furthermore, if the discouraged adolescents feel their lives are moving too fast for them to keep up, adventure offers another means to regain control. If the expectations for academic, social, and athletic performance seem too demanding, and the individuals believe themselves unable to compete in those areas, at least high-risk adventure allows them to name the time and place. Strangely, they experience a new sense of control over their own lives even as they give up their ability and effort as ways to accomplish what they want. If success is beyond their grasp when they use ability or effort, they may as well trust their success to luck. Everything already seems beyond their control.

Karen Horney[5] offers an additional view of adolescents' desire for adventure. When young people want to succeed, to master their environment, but after repeated attempts discover they cannot win their goals, they become very

[5] Horney, Karen, *Neurosis and Human Growth. The Struggle Toward Self-Realization* (New York: W. W. Norton, 1970).

discouraged. To try and fail, by any standard of judgment, demoralizes them. They begin to doubt their abilities and overall worth. Soon, many begin making excuses for their embarrassing performances. After enough setbacks, many find that it hurts less if they care less. Succeeding stops being important to them. Striving stops being important to them. Discouraged young people give up the struggle, saying that they are simply not interested in either the goal or the pursuit.

These young people want to stop hurting, so they stop caring. They tell themselves that their goals are unimportant. The desiring or wishing or needing are unimportant. Feelings of well-being or depression are unimportant. Adolescents discount their feelings and wishes until their lives seem to become flat. They can no longer be disappointed, but they also can no longer be pleased. Direction and purpose disappear. A sense of emptiness and waste replaces it. The "Why bother?" approach, once a protective excuse for not trying to perform, now becomes the problem. Their young lives seem boring and pointless. These adolescents need distractions to mark their time and give their days a focus. Having fun becomes important. They do not want anything serious or meaningful; that would only take them back to caring. A little light entertainment will suit. "Munchies," a bit to drink, occasional sex, pills, parties, or driving around just to be doing something provide the right stimulation to these shallow-living individuals.

Barry didn't care. He figured that his parents cared enough for all of them. Since grade one they cared whether he earned good grades in school. His parents expected A's and B's and gave him stern lectures and punishment for anything less. His parents cared about his friends, freely telling Barry which boys came from the "right" families and which were unfit playmates. His parents cared about his public behavior, parading him at church on Sunday mornings and yelling at him Sunday nights if his bike was seen at the "wrong" house by a curious neighbor that afternoon.

Unfortunately for Barry, he was only an average student with a learning disability that made reading an unpleasant chore. He had friends from families that his parents preferred he avoid. Barry felt the severe disappointment in his father's eyes when he read the report cards. Barry was ashamed that he was letting his family down. By age thirteen, he stopped trying to make good grades. He stopped participating in class. He stopped handing in his homework and studying for tests. He started cutting classes and spent many hours in the principal's office waiting for his mother to arrive for another conference and then take him home. At age fourteen he noticed a traveling carnival camped near his home and went over to have a look. The show stayed for two months, and Barry worked as a handyman for them. He didn't knock himself out but helped with odd jobs. No one asked him about his grades or his friends or his future. Barry enjoyed working with strangers who had no past and asked very little of him. He liked the easy labor and the unpredictable excitement of the carnival atmosphere. Drunks picked fights with midway men or machinery broke while in use. Barry never returned to school.

Gina did not give a darn about anything. No one in her family ever graduated from high school, so why should she? Bright, quick to learn, curious, and personable, she felt uncomfortable around other children. When she earned A's she felt unhappy because she saw herself as unworthy to receive high marks or her teachers' respect.

For years, Gina's alcoholic father beat and sexually abused her. Her mother would go to work and look the other way. Her older brothers would leave the house filthy, and Gina's job was to keep it clean. She was ashamed of her family, ashamed of her shabby clothes, ashamed of her secret. Gina left school and home at age fifteen for a series of part-time jobs, abortions, marijuana or booze when she could get them, and car accidents. She had no sense of personal worth to permit her to use her abilities and energies well. She believed that she had no right to feel good or succeed. She thought it was her rotten luck to be born into this family. She would not take responsibility for planning her life. She would let it just "happen." Life was an exciting adventure, and Gina saw herself as born to be its victim.

Peer Pressure as Scapegoat

Parents and teachers often overestimate peer groups' power and influence. They hear their adolescents speaking and behaving in new ways. Many times the new thoughts and actions are constructive. Craig never seemed interested in his studies before. Although he was bright, he did not like studying, and he earned C's through the middle school grades. Moving into high school, he found himself in classes with a different set of young people. These people seemed to work purposefully in class, turn in first-rate assignments, and take school seriously. Craig respected this group and began adopting their educational values and habits. He wanted to win their approval and acceptance. Craig's parents marveled at his sudden interest in school, his choosing homework instead of TV after dinner, and his Honor Roll report cards. His parents could only shake their heads in pleasure and credit Craig's turnaround to the positive influence of peer pressure.

Other times, young people show new unconstructive attitudes and behaviors. One group of honor students decided to relieve the boredom of a long Friday night with a little innovative recreation. They drove to a local dairy farm, parked the car off the road, climbed the post fence, and located several cows sleeping while standing upright. The boys proceeded to "tip" the resting animals onto their sides. The disoriented cows began crying loudly. Nearby lights went on. An hour later the students were at police headquarters facing fines for trespassing and possible property damage. When their parents arrived, they looked at their children and then at one another, muttering, "My child would have never been so brazen as to pull a stunt like this without the influence of peer pressure!"

For better or worse, adult influence lessens during adolescence while the impact of peer opinions increases. Adolescents want to separate emotionally from their parents. They want to think and act independently. Accordingly, young people try things they have never attempted before and think thoughts they have never imagined until now.

The directions that these thoughts and behaviors take, however, are occasionally wasteful, unproductive, or even self-destructive. Mistakes contribute positively to learning how to be oneself and how to become a mature, responsible adult. For this to happen, the idea or act that falls short must be reevaluated and revised before being attempted again or discarded. The young people seeking an answer to a humdrum evening only to find themselves in police custody must ask themselves if a few moments' excitement justified the embarrassment of being caught, the financial cost of paying damages, or the endless hassles they would surely receive from their distrusting parents once they left the station house. Was the action worth the loss of their parents' respect for their good judgment, or the immorality of deliberately harming another person's possessions?

Most decide the adventure was not worth the cost and choose a more constructive alternative the next time. Even if these young people had not been caught in the act, they would have had to face the cost of the consequences to their own values and self-respect.

Many parents too quickly blame the group for their children's unfortunate behavior. They cite peer pressure as the responsible agent instead of holding the individual adolescents fully accountable for their own actions. Peer pressure becomes a convenient scapegoat. Sadly, this approach clouds the issue. A more effective view would be to ask, "Why is my youngster drawn to this influence?"

Looking behind the behavior to the motive directing it means understanding the cause, not merely its symptoms. Adolescents choose friends who meet certain needs. What need does this behavior meet? Adolescents act with the group because they seek excitement, creative expression, fellowship, or ways to fill dead time because they lack purpose in their lives. On the other hand, a troubling behavior may simply represent a silly, one-time-only lapse of sound judgment.

Acting with the group in destructive ways meets many needs. Well-liked and well-bred Sue had a friend, Ruthie. Ruthie shoplifted, but authorities seldom caught her stealing. She liked to impress friends with her daring. She enjoyed the feeling of control when she "beat the officials." She loved the excitement of achieving the risky. If Ruthie suspected that someone had seen her, she replaced the pilfered item and slowly left the store or bought a nearby item. Scarves, makeup, costume jewelry went from display counter into pockets, cuffs, or an open purse. Sue often "shopped" with Ruthie, but she never took anything herself or accepted gifts from Ruthie. Sue confided to her mother about Ruthie's problem. Sue's mother could not understand why her sweet daughter remained friends with a thief or why Sue dared to accompany Ruthie on her shopping trips.

What needs did Sue meet with this behavior? Perhaps Sue was a loyal friend who wanted to help Ruthie stop a criminal practice. On the other hand, maybe Ruthie did what Sue thought. Ruthie may have been the vehicle for Sue's own unexpressed anger and fears. Sue saw herself as a refined and upright person unable to permit herself public misbehavior, but she could accept this misbehavior in Ruthie. She may even have encouraged it. Looking at the surface, Sue's mother thought Ruthie controlled Sue. The mother blamed peer pressure when the police finally collared Ruthie *and* Sue for shoplifting.

For sixteen-year-old Karen, dealing in drugs meant ready pocket money and a large number of people eager to see her each week. Karen valued this group's acceptance. She believed that her parents never really liked her personality and ideas. Karen also believed that members of more re-spectable peer groups considered her manner and attitude disgusting. Karen had thought there was something wrong with her since she was old enough to dress herself in the blue jeans and T-shirts she preferred to the party dresses her mother neatly hung for her in the closet. She con-sidered herself unworthy of love or real friendship. Be-longing to the drug group by whatever means meant that at least some people desired her company, even if it lasted only as long as to exchange goods and get stoned.

When parents scapegoat peer pressure, they miss the point. They would understand their children better if they looked beneath the behavior to the underlying needs. Everyone wants the good opinion of others. When others like and accept you, it is easier to like and accept yourself. Adolescents seek intimacy, support, and love wherever they can find it. They find excitement, ways of expressing their own confusion or anger, and acceptance. Peer pressure does not make adolescents act in antisocial or destructive ways. Adolescents, instead, select those peers who will allow them to express their real selves, gain the security of belonging, and feel the OK-ness that comes with being a group member.

In addition, research supports the notion that adolescents do not solely follow their friends' lead when deciding how to act.[6] Adolescents take their cues selectively, depending on the question or problem they face. Investigators found that in day-to-day matters such as clothing style, attendance at social events, or whether to drink alcoholic beverages at parties, adolescents tended to listen to their friends. In areas with major implications for their future lives such as how to spend their money, selecting school courses, and deciding on careers, young people tended to seek their parents' advice. One-third of the adolescents in this study expressed uncertainty about which group to consult about intimate interpersonal or sexual concerns.

Perhaps most important, when the investigators compared their 1960 data with 1976 data, they found a significant loss of parental influence and a shift toward peer influence in all areas. More young people today are looking to their friends for advice about intimate and long-range issues than ever before.

As our society in the 1960's and 1970's highly rewarded individualism, adolescents viewed seeking parental advice as shamefully dependent behavior. Autonomy to young people meant acting in accordance with one's own or one's peers' views. Listening to parents' advice seemed like stepping backward into childhood. Acting with peers permitted meeting independence needs.

[6] Sebald, Hans, and White, Becky, "Teenagers' Divided Reference Groups: Uneven Alignment with Parents and Peers," *Adolescence 15,* (60, 1980, Winter): 979–984.

Learning Leadership

Young people want to be successful. They want to know how to act like adults. They want to say and do the right things. They want to be able to act independently and to have life and events work out the way they want. Yet, at the same time, teens know they lack the information, skills, attitudes, and confidence to really make it in the world. One cannot one day be a child relying on parents and teachers to spell out how to do things right and the next day know how to act effectively as a mature individual. Maturity does not arrive wrapped in bright paper and ribbons on one's sixteenth, seventeenth, or eighteenth birthday.

Learning how to act properly and effectively in the world takes time and much trial and error. Becoming an adult takes a lot of experience, and it takes learning how to do it better next time. Gradually gaining information about the way the world works and how one should act in it helps young people feel more self-confident. Slowly building the skills to act successfully also makes young people feel more self-confident. Through all kinds of positive achievements, teens come to know themselves as mature and competent individuals truly able to make their own decisions and live happily with the results.

Peers can influence each other to achieve in positive ways. The Boy Scouts and church youth groups have relied on this belief for years. Community service projects are required for Scouts to reach the respected Eagle rank. Taking food, clothes, and toys to needy families at Christmas and throughout the year and visiting hospitalized members of the community are typical youth group activities.

Likewise, friends who believe that performing well in school is important encourage each other to study hard, to prepare their assignments carefully, and to participate actively in class. No one friend will want to disappoint the others by not doing his or her best in the classroom. School success is an important value that these friends share. Even if a few of the group would like to stop working so hard, they don't want to look bad in front of their friends by being unprepared or turning in sloppy papers.

The same holds true for leadership activities. Some groups of friends think it important to act as leaders in school activities. They count among their friends the newspaper editor, the yearbook editor, the student government heads, club president, varsity cheerleaders, and team captains. They encourage each other to run for class office. They help each other make campaign posters and practice their routines for tryouts. They applaud each other as they take key positions in school activities. These friends like knowing other student leaders because it makes them all feel special and important.

Positive peer influence can provide the youth leadership to stop fights, settle disputes, and solve problems between other teens. Project SMART (School Mediators' Alternative Resolution Team) is operating in several New York City high schools. It comprises groups of teens trained in listening and problem-solving skills. When rumors arise of tension or really bad feelings between persons or groups in the school, the principal calls Project SMART members to meet with the angry students and help them work out their differences through talking and problem-solving rather than violence.

Teens in Project SMART and other peer counseling groups include student leaders, nerds, jocks, punks, hard rockers, and preppies. They are from different backgrounds and different neighborhoods. What they have in common is the desire to help other students express their feelings, look at options, and reach decisions. They learn to listen carefully and help others solve problems. They do not give advice, and they do not break confidences unless a life is in danger.

Programs such as Project SMART depend on the ability of teens to learn mature problem-solving skills and help other teens in trouble. One of the reasons teens can help is that they have deep feelings of caring and understanding for other people. Peer counseling or Project SMART training gives teens the skills and supervision they need to act effectively on what they naturally want to do anyway.

In addition, peer counselors are teens wanting their own independence. Wanting to be separate and apart is one need. Wanting to be close and supportive of another is a very different need. Teens can learn listening skills and the objective yet empathic ability to truly understand what another person is saying and meaning without becoming overinvolved.

Conclusion

Achievement opportunities during adolescence provide chances for young people to develop important attitudes and skills. They learn how to get along with people, how to master important skills, and how to make mature decisions. They will achieve in positive ways if they have an interest in the activity and the abilities to accomplish it, are willing to spend the energy, have the chance to get involved, and are willing to wait for a later reward. If adolescents fear that they won't succeed, they can use a strategy to avoid the feeling of failure. Others might seek different ways and means to meet their needs. Adventure can offer delightful recreation or a destructive excuse for not learning the important attitudes and skills necessary for a responsible adulthood.

Chapter **IV**

Adolescent Sexuality

Many adults and professionals working with teenagers, as well as teens themselves, view adolescent sexuality as a behavior akin to using illegal drugs or driving recklessly. Some think all these behaviors are morally wrong, dangerous to the persons involved, and signs of young people's rebellion against adults. Others think sex, drugs, and driving happen together in a cause and effect way: drugs and cars lead to sex. Still others believe adolescent sexuality, drug use, and driving signal disturbed and delinquent young people.

Disapproving adults and teens have a point. Adolescent sexuality, drug use, and reckless driving do have things in common. Each behavior represents a way in which young people can look and act like adults. Adults control their own sexuality and can express it whenever and with whomever they please. The TV commercials and magazine ads say this loud and clear. Their own parents' behavior say it, too. Likewise, adults freely buy and use prescription and over-the-counter drugs or alcohol without answering to anyone. Adults have cars and the freedom to come and go that cars provide.

Each behavior also represents a legal position. In many states, adolescents must reach a specified age before they are legally permitted to marry without their parents' consent. Adolescents must be a certain age before they are allowed by law to buy alcoholic beverages, and before they are eligible to apply for a driver's license. Having sex with a legally defined "minor" means breaking a law either by contributing to the delinquency of a minor or by statutory rape. The law says the older one is, the more right one has to become involved in these activities. In that way, the activities themselves become symbols of maturity.

Finally, sex, drugs, and driving are all very difficult to handle responsibly. The highly charged emotions involved often make calm, rational decision-making about how to use them impossible. Each activity means more to the individuals than the behavior itself. Questions come forward about identity, personal values, what friends and parents will think, the importance of appearing independent and mature, as well as the unexpressed angers and fears that can be played out indirectly through irresponsible sex, drug use, or careless driving. Moreover, these acts have overwhelming consequences; what individuals do in a few minutes can drastically affect the rest of their lives.

On the other hand, disapproving adults and adolescents miss an important point. Unlike drug use or car abuse, adolescent sexuality represents normal, positive, and wholesome behavior. Here attitudes and behaviors grow that fulfill the sense of self and societal role. Each person has a definite gender—male or female. This gender identity is an essential facet in the way we see ourselves and in the way others see and treat us. Adolescents use their sexuality in halting, exploratory ways to understand themselves and others, physically, emotionally, and socially. Becoming at ease with their own sexuality means gradually becoming responsible, satisfied adults. Sexual development during adolescence leads toward building a full, mature personality. In contrast, drug use and careless driving often spell ways to avoid facing responsibilities and mature decision-making. Aware and responsible sexuality helps young people to face directly their personal values, their relationships with others, and the outcomes of their choices.

The Role of Sexuality in Adolescence

Adolescence is a time when individuals define themselves. Discovering who they are as male or female persons enacts a normal, important part of their whole identity. Coming to terms with their sexuality—learning to be comfortable with their bodies, accepting their new physical responsiveness, trying out new social behaviors, and noticing the way others respond to this special facet of their personalities—can be a confusing affair. Never before in their lives has an aspect so personal and private become so public.

Developing the abilities to have intimate relationships counts as a major task of adolescence. Young people have families who will love and care for them no matter what happens. Parents give love without conditions. They feel deep affection for their children and want to help them make their lives meaningful. Grandparents, aunts, uncles, and cousins enter their lives, exchanging the same concern and fondness because they share a family tradition. In adolescence, a difference appears. Young people feel pressure to begin associations with friends apart from their families. Independence becomes an important quality. Now adolescents must win and keep friends on the basis of the same interests, enjoyable personalities, trust, and mutual caring. They must be willing to open up private fears and troubling questions to their friends. They must also be willing to listen kindly and without judgment to their friends' concerns. Adolescents learn to develop emotional closeness to persons who were once strangers.

Adolescents frequently "fall in love." The sense of fullness and energy that comes with romantic ties feels wonderful. In addition, the special emotional closeness that the couple share meets many needs. The emotional bond teaches individuals about the actual give and take of mature relationships. Working out misunderstandings, learning to express loving and hurt feelings to another person honestly yet caringly, finding ways to be an individual as well as part of a pair all take time and experience.

What is more, falling in love typifies another way to define oneself. No longer one solitary person, the individual becomes part of a couple. For instance, Sue reflected the way Jack saw himself and the way he wanted others to know him. She was intelligent, cute, preppy, and popular; therefore, by going together as a couple, Jack also became intelligent, good-looking, preppy, and popular.

Many adolescents seek to complete their picture of themselves by falling in love with a person who has the qualities they wish they themselves had. Wade was always a serious-minded A student, shy and a loner, but he found light-hearted girls very attractive. When Janet accepted his invitation to go to the movies, Wade rejoiced. Well-liked, pretty, a bundle of energy and smiles, Janet had many friends. She studied only in order to be promoted and not appear too foolish. Wade and Janet had fun together. Janet gained an interesting boyfriend while Wade escaped the academic pressures and had the chance to meet many new people.

Intimate relationships include physical as well as emotional closeness. Adolescents learn how to express their physical selves during these years. Puberty brings physical changes in height, weight, and muscles. Body proportions change. The outward signs of maturity become readily visible.

The greatest changes, however, happen on the inside.

Hormonal changes responsible for the external sexual characteristics also influence the body's responsiveness to sexual cues. Adolescent women suddenly develop a keen interest in young men. Only yesterday they could not have cared less if they attracted a young man's attention. Today the young women plan, gossip, and play out awkward flirtations to capture a young man's eye. A little later, young men begin taking an interest in their female classmates.

Adolescents experience definite physical reactions to thoughts about members of the opposite sex and to activities with them. The sensations for some are pleasantly mild. For others, the sensations seem overpoweringly urgent. These physical tensions and their expression are new and real.

At first, adolescents' bodies lead their minds and emotions. Their physical awareness quickly becomes the most important message they hear. The results often disturb young people. Many young men feel as if they cannot control their excitement and dread the possibility of having others notice their arousal. Young women find themselves privately exploring their bodies, strongly "turned on" by male recording stars or fantasizing about their male teachers.

The physical equipment for adult sexuality exists in young adolescents, but the social permission to engage in sexual behavior does not. Young people today stand financially or vocationally unready to marry. Many long years of formal education and training lie ahead. Assuming too many responsibilities at this time could short-circuit life plans and ambitions.

Nor are the young people's emotional experiences ready for adult sexuality. Young people are not emotionally capable of understanding, developing, or maintaining an adult sexual relationship. Relating to another on this most inti-

mate level requires a balance between holding on to a separate identity and giving it up in complete openness to the
other. To keep the balance means first truly knowing and
understanding oneself. Confident in this knowledge, one
can risk vulnerability to another without completely losing
one's uniqueness. Developing this confident self-awareness takes time and experience. Young adolescents do not
yet have this solid sense of self. They are only beginning
to learn who they are and what they believe. For them, too
early sexual involvement risks losing their initiative, independence, and search for self as they give all to their
partner. Alternately, they risk holding back so much of
themselves emotionally for fear of losing everything to the
other that they can never really know deep sharing and
trust.

In early adolescence, young people have sexual awak-
ening without sexual intelligence. Biologically, they are
ready to begin sexual relationships. Emotionally, intellectually, socially, and in every other way they are not ready.
This difference in time between awareness and its approved expression creates great inner tension for young
people. During adolescence they prepare themselves to become adults capable of emotional and sexual intimacy by
trying out different sexual attitudes and behaviors.

Adolescent Sexuality as Exploratory Behavior

Adolescents behave in sexually exploratory ways. They
aim at self-definition. Adolescents use sex as one way of
searching for their own values, attitudes, and styles of behaving as males or females.

When adults speak of sex, they usually refer to sexual
intercourse or coitus. Sexual behavior includes more than
genital-to-genital contact. Fantasizing about being with at-

tractive individuals of the opposite sex also represents a sexual behavior. Making and holding eye contact with someone you find attractive constitutes a sexual act. In our society, holding another person's gaze is an intimate action. When strangers look each other in the eye, they engage in an aggressive, perhaps even hostile, behavior. They visually enter another's space and, in a way, invade that person's privacy. This society teaches its children to look away quickly, not to stare or act rudely like this. So when an individual seeks eye contact and the other person holds the gaze, they may be saying, "It is okay for you to be intimate with me in this way."

Holding hands or standing close together in our culture sometimes signals sexual behaviors. Again, the intimacy of two people sharing their personal space suggests a trust and rapport between them. People say many things by holding hands. The cold, damp, stiff hand speaks of an inexperienced, shy person. Surprising squeezes and tickles speak of an enthusiastic, playful person. The strong, firm hand speaks of confidence and assurance. Fingers of two hands laced together suggest still more intimate behavior between the persons. Many conventions and styles of hand-holding mean that young people try out different ways, judging how they feel when they do it and how the other person responds to the changes.

For many young people, what looks like sexual behavior to outsiders may not mean anything erotic to them. Going steady, fall in love, flirting, kissing, and hand-holding may be only social behaviors without any sexual intentions. Society, parents, and peers expect young people to find members of the opposite sex attractive. Becoming part of a couple symbolizes an adult behavior and brings the pair approval and recognition. Gestures such as walking hand-in-hand, coy teasing, and even kissing "Goodnight" may be symbols alone, not more sexually stimulating to those involved than waving "See you!" to Great Aunt Martha. For many young people, the appearance value of this adultlike behavior is the important thing. They go through the motions because this is the ritual they see older people perform. For many, sexual motives do not play a part. Although fantasizing, making eye contact, and hand-holding are not always sexual acts, caressing, lengthy kissing, petting, intercourse, and masturbation can be nothing less. Many ways of expressing sexual attraction exist, yet sex remains an exciting mystery to adolescents. They see photos in magazines and bedroom scenes in popular movies, they read racy passages in paperback books, but they are unsure how to put it all together. Their friends talk about making love, but very few young people know how to begin. Society makes clear the expectations of what it means to be a man or a woman in this culture. Young people quickly ask, "How?" when the important question they should be asking is, "Is this what I really want for myself now?"

Sex cannot be separated from the individuals expressing it. Sex means more than knowing erotic moves and Latin names for the genitals. Sexual behavior includes the values and attitudes that the individuals bring with them. Adolescents are not always certain what they believe. Sometimes action brings chances to look closely at one's behaviors and one's feelings about those behaviors. Lana, fifteen years old, wanted to be thought of as attractive and sophisticated. One Saturday on a trip to a local college library to complete research for a history paper, she met a young man. Josh, a sophomore at the college, asked her to go to a party with him the next weekend. Ecstatic, Lana eagerly agreed to go. When she told her parents about the events at the library, they seemed reluctant. They said he was too old for Lana. "Nonsense!" she replied. "We had a lot to say to one another. He thought I was interesting." Her parents hesitantly gave their okay for the date. Once at the party, Lana noticed many couples paired off in corners, intensely kissing and petting. She suddenly felt very uncomfortable, like a Peeping Tom seeing things meant to be private. Later, when Josh's hands started rubbing her back, Lana became tight and stiff. She asked Josh to take her home right then. Lana's discomfort told her she was not ready for this type of behavior. Maybe she would never be ready for public sex. She wanted to be worldly, but her values would not allow her to become sexually active like this now.

Patrick wanted to feel like a man. He was seventeen, and his friends teased him about his innocence. He liked girls but didn't feel very confident around them. He could talk to girls sitting near him in classes or in the cafeteria. He had even gone to the movies and football games with young ladies. But Patrick never did more than hold hands or give a hasty good night kiss. One day his best friend's cousin, Rita, visited from out of town. Rita, also seventeen, had many boyfriends back home.

Patrick and Rita went to a football game. Later, Rita persuaded Patrick to drive to a wooded area ten miles from town to see the changing October leaves. She told Patrick how good-looking he was, how attractive he was, how excited she felt near him. She looked into his eyes and began to touch him. Patrick was stunned. Then he was curious. She encouraged him to lie down in the woods, undress, and explore each other's bodies.

As they drove back several hours later, Patrick started feeling slightly sick to his stomach. By evening, his illness turned into sadness. Patrick felt unhappy about his sexual involvement with Rita. He hardly knew her, but he knew he did not love her. James, his best friend, trusted him. Patrick thought he had let James down by his selfish behavior. What would his parents think of him if they knew? Would they lose respect for him? He even felt sorry for Rita, who acted in such a personal way with practically a stranger. Patrick behaved in a way his peers expected, but he learned after the fact that he did not want to act that way.

High school sweethearts, Jessica and Tom met in eighth grade, and by ninth grade everybody knew they were a couple. Sincere, honest, hardworking, and ambitious, they both wanted to earn high grades and go on to college. They cared deeply for each other. They shared their joys, secrets, fears, and future plans. Although they felt a strong physical attraction for one another, they never became more sexually intimate than standing close, kissing, and mildly petting until they reached age seventeen. Both Jessica and Tom respected their parents' traditional values. They believed sex before marriage was wrong, and they had been conscientious about not going "too far." Yet they also knew they loved one another deeply, and they wanted to enrich their relationship through physical intimacy. With thoughtful planning and open discussions about their situation, they decided to begin making love whenever they could find the time and the privacy. Jessica and Tom decided in a clear-eyed way to use contraceptives and begin a new way to communicate their love through sexual activity. They did, and for them the decision felt like the right one.

Through such incidents, these young people learned more about their values concerning sex and relationships. They acted in sexual ways and discovered more about themselves. Sex is only one aspect of a full personality. Personalities, not sex, form relationships. People build relationships on shared affection, trust, caring, and emotional intimacy. The young people learned that sex is not a satisfying alternative to having a relationship. It comes after the love, not before. Relationships give sex its meaning and significance. Without this context, Lana and Patrick found sex empty and discouraging. For Jessica and Tom in a full relationship, it had a special meaning.

Adolescents look for ways to develop and maintain satisfying, mature, realistic relationships. They move beyond hero worship, "crushes," and puppy love. They learn how to express love and affection, mutual caring, and respect. They learn how to do this through trial and error, testing, and seeing what agrees with their attitudes and values and what does not.

In this regard, adolescents today have a rougher time learning about their sexual selves than did their parents and teachers. Twenty years ago society encouraged different behaviors. The rules clearly stated: sex only within marriage. An unwritten rule said: If you're going to have sex, you had better be a man and do it with a not-very-nice woman. The double standard reigned. No one was supposed to have sex. Men did. Nice women did not. Following this clear-cut prescription was easy. Individuals did not have to guess, regret, or evaluate their values. Today, a popular sexual standard says "permissiveness with affection." If your personal morals permit premarital sex, and if you and your partner care for each other, having sex is okay. This expectation means more testing, more questions, and more upsets for young people.

Adolescents feel the social pressure to become sexually active before they become emotionally, intellectually, or financially ready. The statistics show a high percentage of young people involved in sexual activities. One study[1] finds

[1] Hass, Aaron, *Teenage Sexuality. A Survey of Teenage Sexual Behavior* (New York: Macmillan, 1979).

that in 1979, 31 percent of the girls and 43 percent of the boys had had sexual intercourse by age sixteen.By age eighteen, 56 percent of the girls and 56 percent of the boys had had sexual intercourse. One-half of the unmarried women age nineteen and four out of five males had had sexual intercourse.

Even though more adolescents today than yesterday use birth control, nearly two-thirds of the adolescent girls having sex said they either never used contraception or did so every now and then in a careless way. Fifty-one percent of the teenage girls interviewed said they did not think they could get pregnant.[2] The increase in adolescent pregnancies, childbirth, and abortions represents some of the high emotional and financial costs of teenage sexuality. The decisions grow more difficult, and the costs are much greater today than ever before.

Why Adolescents Become Sexually Active

Physical Reasons   Many factors enter young people's decisions to become sexually active. Physically, young people become able to behave sexually after puberty. Their bodies have grown in adult ways. The physical maturity sometimes builds a very real body tension. Spending the tension feels good. Some adolescents have sex because their bodies feel excited and alive when they do. Whether through masturbation or sexual activity with another person, adolescents receive physical pleasure from sexual acts.

Jessica and Tom found another physical reason for becoming sexually active. Their relationship grew stronger every year, and they shared a genuine love. They were seventeen years old and wanted to deepen their communication and commitment. They deliberately chose to ex-

---

[2] "Teenage Pregnancies: The Problem That Hasn't Gone Away," Alan Guttmacher Institute, Planned Parenthood Affiliate, cited in *The Daily Press,* March 3, 1981).

pand their relationship to include sexual intercourse. By using contraception in their plans, they acted responsibly. They knowingly chose to begin a sexual part of their relationship and believed they acted with maturity and consideration for each other.

Social Reasons   Many reasons having little to do with sex and a lot to do with defining an identity lead young people to become sexually active. For adolescents, sexuality expresses another part of their emerging personalities. They have adultlike bodies and responses to sexual excitement, but they look to become at ease with their maleness or femaleness. They try to discover who they are, what they believe and value, how to act, and where they're going. Becoming a sexual person represents a small part of the larger search for self.

Sex in adolescence provides an identity to individuals unsure about who they are. Steve, age fifteen, was concerned about his personality. He wondered if his ideas made sense and if he was interesting or entertaining enough to attract friends. He did not know what he had to offer others, and he felt that he was probably the least important member of his group. He met Sandy at a school dance. She charmed him with her quick smile and hearty laugh. She enjoyed people, and they seemed to enjoy her. When Steve and Sandy began dating, Steve's view of himself changed. Now he was part of a couple. Sandy brought the easy warmth to make others feel at ease. Steve was no longer "boring Steve." He became part of a fun-loving couple. The world saw him as 50 percent of this winning combination, and that became the way he saw himself. Now he had a definite likable identity.

In addition, sex stands as a symbol of adult maturity. Nita, age fourteen, wanted to be grown-up. She thought her parents overprotective and old-fashioned. They did not like for her to go out on school nights. They stood over her as she completed her homework. They did not like her making her own decisions about friends, smoking, or drinking. Nita and her boyfriend began behaving sexually so that Nita could tell herself that she was truly a mature woman rather than the little girl her parents kept forcing her to be.

A Way of Solving Nonsexual Problems   For many adolescents, sexual activity becomes a way to solve problems that have nothing to do with sex.[3] For Mary Ann, having sex meant a way to rebel against her strict, controlling parents. They constantly criticized her behavior, her friends, her ideas, and her appearance. They wanted to know where she was and what she was doing every moment she was out of the house. The more quiet she became, the more vigorously they pried. When Mary Ann returned home from a date, her parents grilled her with questions. Mary Ann deeply resented this intrusion into her privacy and swore that her parents could not run her life. She began sleeping with her boyfriend to "get even" with her parents and to prove who was really in charge.

Other adolescents use sex to express anger. When Jack was eleven his mother divorced his father, and she began seeing other men a year later. She left Jack with a babysitter and went out on the town. She and Jack had spent much time together during the uproar of the separation and divorce, but now she had little time for her son. All her energies seemed aimed toward attracting and pleasing a parade of strangers. Jack loved his mother very much and craved some of her attention. When his mother began a

[3] Kennedy, Eugene. *Sexual Counseling* (New York: The Seabury Press, 1977).

new job, she had still less time for Jack. Slowly, Jack began to feel anger toward her. The anger scared and confused him because he could not understand how he could both adore and despise the same person.

While Jack denied the anger he felt toward his mother, it appeared in his relationships with his girlfriends. As an adolescent Jack had good looks and charm, with a smooth and convincing line. He would meet and flatter a young woman, date her twice, then tell her how much he loved her and needed her. Next, he would press for a sexual relationship, telling her how attractive she was and how much he loved her. After she gave in, Jack never asked her out again. For their part, the girls viewed him as a challenge. Each wanted to change this Romeo into a steady, sincere boyfriend. In truth, Jack never cared much for any of his girlfriends. He used them as an indirect way of expressing his anger toward his mother.

Escaping pressure from elsewhere sometimes leads to a sexual relationship. Tammy had many responsibilities at home. At age fifteen she cooked breakfast for her two younger brothers, dressed them, got herself ready and off to school, cleaned house in the afternoon and the kitchen after dinner, then did her homework. Every other day, she washed the laundry. Tammy was always exhausted. Both her parents had jobs and felt too tired or busy to help her with the chores. They told her this work was good preparation for her future marriage and household responsibilities.

When Tammy met Alex, she liked him at once. A thoughtful person, he seemed to care for her. Tammy had never felt such kindness from anyone before in her life, and her time with Alex became a wonderful vacation from the never-ending duties at home. The relationship began to mean everything to her. When Alex suggested they make love, Tammy paused a moment and then agreed. If Alex wanted to have sex, okay with her. He had given her so much affection; now she could give him something in return. She knew she did not love him, but she felt grateful. Their time together became a haven safe from the demands elsewhere.

Becoming sexually active can also be a defense against loneliness. Carol, age fourteen, didn't like herself. Her older sister was smart, whereas Carol thought herself stupid. Her sister was attractive, but Carol considered herself plain. Her sister always had many friends, but Carol never felt comfortable with people. In high school Carol felt like a failure. Poor grades, few friends, and no dates meant everyone knew Carol was a loser. She wanted to become part of the life around her but always hung back, afraid that others would laugh at her if she asked to participate.

Carol felt lonely and invisible until she met her girlfriend's older brother. Harry, age twenty, worked as a mechanic in a local garage. For several weeks he did not notice the new face around home with his sister. One day he grabbed a beer from the refrigerator, turned and saw Carol. He winked and walked out. Carol immediately felt a rush of love for Harry. He was the first young man to give her any attention. The wink led to "Hello" and finally to a date. When Harry and Carol went to the movies, he put his hand on her leg. Carol jumped in surprise, but then relaxed. Harry sensed her consent and went still further. Carol had never known any relationship with a boy before this, and being with Harry felt wonderful to her. For the first time in her life she felt pretty, desirable, and appreciated. With Harry, she no longer felt lonely or ugly, unhappy or unimportant. The sex did not matter to her. At least with Harry, she did not feel like a loser.

For a few adolescents, sex can be a form of suicide.

Beth, age fourteen, thought herself worthless. Her parents and brothers always called her stupid and ugly. Since age nine she had cooked and cleaned the house daily, but her parents never showed appreciation for her efforts. They constantly found fault with her work and cruelly belittled her in front of her friends. Soon the friends stopped visiting her home. Feeling depressed and discouraged, Beth began cutting classes. She failed every subject in ninth grade because of excessive absences and uncompleted assignments. She felt that nothing mattered. She did not deserve happiness, now or ever.

Wanting to run away but with no place to go, Beth began spending time with a kind-hearted neighbor. A divorcee, age twenty-six, the neighbor often entertained men callers. Soon she began inviting male friends to visit Beth, too. Beth went to bed with these men as if she were in a fog. She gave in to whatever they asked of her because she wanted to die and cared little about what happened to her. When they were finished, she felt cheap, used, and even more worthless. The more roughly the men treated her, the closer Beth felt to death.

A last way in which adolescents become sexually active as a way to solve nonsexual problems is through molestation, rape, or incest. Many adolescents are victims of child abuse. Young people trust family members and family friends to treat them safely and protectively. Yet many adults take advantage of this trusting relationship to fondle or molest young people under the guise of affection or good-natured teasing. Relatives or friends can take advantage of the opportunity for intimate physical contact with a young person. Step-siblings and family friends have fewer incest taboos to break by this behavior. Many times the young people are so inexperienced that they do not realize they are being sexually abused. Others do understand what is happening, but they are too afraid of being hurt worse if they protest or fight the molester. In other cases the young people love the person abusing them and want to protect that person from public disapproval, humiliation, or a criminal charge. Sometimes the offended adolescents want to protect the feelings of others involved, such as a mother, grandmother, or aunt. Others continue the practice of sexual involvement with relatives or family friends in exchange for gifts or special favors. Adolescent males also experience sexual molestation by relatives or older friends. Most sexually abused young people remain silent about the incidents and suffer alone.

For young people, sexual activity can be a way to express the problems of growing up. Sex provides a behavior by which to act out questions about who they are and what they stand for. Sexual activity can be a way to express rebellion against strict, controlling parents or anger at persons they otherwise deeply love. Sex can be a way to feel less lonely or less worthless. Sex can offer a way to escape from pressures elsewhere in their lives. It can also be a way to appear mature. Sexual activity in adolescence does not have to be erotic. It is often a mask hiding more troubling, unsettled issues.

Peer Pressure and Adolescent Sexuality

Peer pressure acts as an important influence encouraging young people to become sexually active. Adolescents look to the group to set rules for correct social behavior. When the peer group says, "Sexual activity is the right thing to do," group members feel the expectation to become sexually active, whether they are ready or not.

Sexuality is an area of confusion and uncertainty for most young people. They know sex involves important adult behaviors and fosters many exciting emotions. They know the body parts used in sexual intercourse and the basic mechanics of how they work. They see the respect given friends who seem expert in these matters and the confident assurance these friends show in their relationships.

Young people, however, do not understand how to develop and maintain relationships in which sexuality can enhance communication between two deeply caring individuals. Not all realize that a strong relationship is a crucial part of satisfying sexuality. They do not understand the extent and complexity of their feelings about sex. Adolescents do not recognize how values about sex can influence how good they feel about themselves or how worthless and used they feel about a sexual experience. Sexuality becomes a badge of maturity to young people, and they fear looking ridiculous to their friends if they act ignorant about sex or express hesitance about becoming sexually active.

As a result, many young people listen to their friends talk and feel left out if they do not start having sexual relations. Having sex seems like the thing to do. The less young people really understand about sex, the more open they become to their friends' influence about how to act and when to begin. Since adolescents know very little about sex and its implications, peer pressure fills the gap and encourages this behavior.

Particularly for young men ages fifteen to sixteen, peers expect them to have sex. Adolescent boys, eager to prove their manhood, use sexual activity as a symbol of their new maturity. At this age young men are ready to kiss-and-tell, and they often seek quick relationships with young women they do not truly love in order to meet the masculinity requirement that their friends set. Even if the young men do not press beyond hand-holding and a lingering kiss on the porch steps, the retelling of the event on Monday morning sounds more exciting. Young men admire those who speak of their sexual experiences because the whole process of sex remains an intriguing mystery. The attention and respect given to sexually sophisticated young men encourages them to continue talking about their amorous adventures. It also encourages more inexperienced fellows to act and become more worldly, or at least talk as if they were. Sexual activity to this group means increased status in their friends' eyes.

Other adolescents go along with their friends' expectations of sexual activity to prevent the group from rejecting them. Denise's girlfriends all had had boyfriends since they were high school sophomores. Once a close circle of girls, her friends now spent most of their time as couples. They giggled about their special intimacies with young men. It seemed as if Denise needed to discuss a sexual adventure if she wanted her friends to listen. Denise valued her friends' company and feared that if she did not begin acting like them and find a boyfriend, the girls would drop her altogether.

When she began dating Bud during her junior year, she felt relieved. Now she could again be included in her friends' plans. Denise made a point of having long, passionate kisses with Bud whenever her friends were nearby so they might witness her new maturity. When her friends began sleeping with their boyfriends and discussing the details afterwards, Denise knew she had a problem. She did not want to become that intimately involved with Bud, but she did not want to lose her place in the group either. She decided to go along with Bud's hesitant request for sexual intercourse in order to keep her friends' interest.

For many adolescents, having sexual relations is an alternative to developing a real relationship. Neil was a handsome eighteen-year-old. Since the age of five his family had told him that he was good-looking. They made allowances for his uncooperative behavior because his face and excuses were so charming. Neil quickly learned how to sweet-talk his teachers into giving him a few more points on his tests and a few days' extension on assignments. He drew many friends with his attractive looks and growing athletic skills.

In high school Neil dated a number of popular girls. He seemed to have a new girlfriend every few months. He developed an effective line that lured many dates into the back seat of his car.

His girlfriends commented later, however, that they never really knew Neil. Physically, yes, he was a skilled lover. As a person, however, he was not really there. Neil knew how to have sexual relations but not how to have a person-to-person relationship. Praised constantly for his appearance and able to get whatever he wanted through guile, Neil never learned to define his real views about subjects or to listen perceptively to anyone else. He did not know how to reveal his innermost thoughts or questions with another person or how to be comfortable listening to theirs. Neil thought that the only things of value he had to offer another person were his appearance and his mechanical expertise in love-making. His inner talents and personality remained undeveloped. Neil believed that sex equaled an intimate relationship. He completely missed the caring emotional bonds that truly loving couples share.

In a different vein, peer pressure affects sexual activity as a way to show power over others. Helen deeply resented her father. As long as she could remember, he and her mother had fought each other. At first the arguments were just loud, but after a while he began beating her mother. Bruised and weakened, Helen's mother never wanted to report the beatings to the police. As unhappy as she was with Helen's father, she felt she would be lost without him. The violent scenes continued, Helen watching terrified from the kitchen corner or hearing the cries of pain coming up through the floorboards in her room. Helen swore to herself that she would never let herself become so dependent on any man that she would take the beatings her mother did.

When Helen entered eleventh grade, her friends began serious dating. They would get together and swap stories about their boyfriends. Helen did not like the idea of seeing young men socially because she carried so much unexpressed anger toward her father. She reasoned, though, that if she had to begin dating in order to remain part of her group, she would do it in a way that would guarantee she was not hurt. In her relationships with young men, Helen always kept her emotional distance. She would slyly tease, then draw back. She would attentively flatter them one day and act coldly indifferent the next. Her boyfriends were understandably confused at these mixed messages. She encouraged them enough to make them return but ignored them enough to keep them uncertain about her true feelings. Helen used sexual behavior to show she was the powerful one, in control of the relationship.

Many adolescents become involved in sexual behavior they really do not want. When asked why, they answer:

"I didn't want to hurt anyone's feelings."
"I felt pressured and afraid not to have sex."
"When we have sex, we don't argue."
"I was high on drugs or alcohol at the time."
"I was afraid the relationship would end if I did not have sex."
"Sex seemed to mean a lot to the other person and it didn't really matter to me."
"I felt I owed it to the other person."

"I felt something was wrong with me if I didn't have sex."

"I wanted to give my love and give encouragement."

"I did not want to seem like a tease."

What these adolescents mean is, "I could not say 'No!'" They lacked the confidence in their own thoughts and values to act on them. Unable to translate their values into actions, they went along with what they thought others expected of them. These adolescents became sexually active because it seemed easier to go along with the others' expectations than to trust themselves and act on their own values.

Role of Peers in Understanding Sexuality

While sexuality is a normal and positive aspect of teenage growth, too often sex becomes the wrong way for unhappy teens to try to solve problems in their lives. Whether they are trying to feel loved and valued for a few minutes or to find a purpose for their lives, sex becomes a tool to help teens feel that their life has meaning and direction.

The Washington Area Improvisational Teen Theatre (WAITT) is a teen group that uses positive peer pressure to encourage young people to stay away from sex and to warn them of the risk of pregnancy. The twelve-member troupe has appeared all over the country before eager high school audiences, which react to their message with interest. Using a catchy beat and a syncopated style, WAITT says, "She didn't think twice . . . now she's suffering the consequences, paying the price." And, "She dropped out of school, she's wasting most of her life. All because of just one night." WAITT also fights the stereotypes that virginity is uncool and that macho men make love to anyone they like. Teens listen to these peers, agreeing with the advice that they might have turned off if it had come from an adult.[4]

Positive peer influence has another role to play here, too. Many times teens use sex to solve other problems because they don't really know how to solve those problems. Friends know when something is wrong with someone they care about, and they can help each other identify and solve the real situation. Then sex as a tool is not needed.

First, helping friends must help their troubled friend see what the real problem is. They need to look at the troubled friend's feelings and thoughts, not just tell the friend that he or she is wrong or crazy to have such feelings and thoughts. If friends are really to help, they must be understanding and not play the roles of judge and jury.

Friends can ask the following questions and listen closely and caringly to the answers:

"Without pretending to yourself or to me, being totally honest, how do you really feel?"

"What thoughts are you having about these feelings?"

"Tell me about the situation in your life that is making you have these emotions? What is happening that upsets you? What is not happening that you wish were happening?"

Have the upset friend look closely at him or herself and what is causing these thoughts and feelings. Just expressing these thoughts and feelings to a caring other person

[4]"The Message: WAITT," Newport News *Daily Press*, March 26, 1987, A4.

can help the upset friend understand him or herself better by identifying uncomfortable and unclear tensions inside. Talking brings many of the issues out into the real world where they can be seen and solved.

Next, the helping friend can help the upset friend look at different solutions to the problem. Let him or her voice as many choices as possible without assistance. When the upset friend can think of no more choices, the helper friends can add still other alternatives.

"What do you want to happen? What do you want to happen in the short run (this week, next week)? What do you want to happen in the long run (next month, next year)?"

"What choices do you have about what to do?" (Brainstorm all the possible ways of solving the problem, from the wild and crazy answers to the plain hard work/no nonsense answers.)

"What is good and bad about each choice? How would each choice affect your life and your thoughts and feelings for better and for worse? Is there a difference in good and bad between the short run and the long run?"

When all the choices and their good and bad points have been discussed, the helper friend can assist the upset friend in deciding which one to try.

"What do you think you're going to do?"
"When are you going to do it?"
"How will you know when it is done?"
"How and when will you know if it works?"

This is the hardest part of problem-solving. Talking is easy compared with really doing something about a bad situation. Problems can take weeks, months, or years to form, and they cannot be solved in a one-shot action. In addition, some bad situations come from other persons' actions, and little can be done to change that situation. Sometimes good solutions do not work the first time they are tried. A small mistake in wording, in timing, or in the persons involved can make the solution seem wrong even when, in fact, it is right.

In short, problem-solving takes patience. Looking for and defining the problem takes time. Finding a decent solution takes time. And putting the solution to work in the real world takes time and the willingness to review and revise plans and actions. Solving problems takes one good step after another rather than expecting one action to solve all difficulties. That is why positive friends are so important. Positive peer pressure can maintain the optimism that things will work out right sooner or later. Positive friends bring the confidence to keep working at the solution one day at a time, day after day, and year after year if necessary. Friends can help each other see what a good plan is, where the good plan went wrong, and how to do it better next time. They can help each other feel truly understood and less afraid of a bad situation.

Finally, positive friends can support each other through events over which they may have little control. Some situations must be waited out, but a different attitude can make the same situation feel less terrible. If family problems, for instance, make teens feel as if they are to blame, good friends can help them see that they may not be at fault and do not have to feel guilty. Without guilt, their attitude and feelings about the situation change. They still do not like it and wish it were different, but they no longer feel so torn up about it.

When teens can learn to solve problems in their lives,

they feel less need to act out sexually. Friends can influence their friends in positive ways to express sex maturely and responsibly when the time is right, rather than to use it as a weapon or a way to escape.

Conclusion

Adolescents want to understand who they are as unique individuals. They develop their personalities by examining and testing their attitudes, values, and behaviors in a variety of situations. They then evaluate which beliefs and acts suit them and which do not. Sexuality represents an aspect of personality that young people explore and seek to understand more fully.

Adolescent sexuality brings young people more self-awareness and greater interaction with others. Learning to feel comfortable with their own bodies and thoughts is a difficult task because young people are physically able to become sexually active years before they are socially or psychologically ready. Many strong and complex emotions involved with sexuality make it possible for adolescents to act in sexual ways for reasons having little or nothing to do with sex. Sex gets mixed up with issues such as independence, power, anger, self-worth, and peer pressure. Meanwhile, young people learn to develop meaningful relationships and wonder how to be truly and wholly themselves with other persons.

Chapter **V**

Adolescents and Loss

Throughout life, people build strong emotional bonds with many others. Relationships grow when people care deeply about each other. People feel good about themselves when spending time with these special persons, knowing they can count on one another for support in difficult hours and for fun when they feel light-hearted. People develop trust in the ties between them. Young people experience trust in themselves when others show confidence in their judgment. Involved in meaningful relationships, young people feel more able to solve problems and try out new mature behaviors.

Sometimes certain things gain importance. The flower pressed in the dictionary reminds one young woman about her exciting prom evening. The photograph, the key ring, the three-line note from Dad saying how proud he was of you all hold special places in a person's life.

People also attach great meaning to their goals and dreams. They plan for future activities and work toward tomorrow's career. They begin studying to be a doctor, and they pick out clothes for the Christmas party. They can practically see themselves walking to the podium at graduation, receiving the hard-earned diploma, and shaking the principal's hand.

Frequently, our most meaningful connections endure. Relationships last and grow stronger. Valued tokens stay with us and keep on bringing warm, happy feelings. Plans and hours of preparation work out the way we intended. Sometimes people get what they want and feel as if nothing can stop the good feelings or end today's sense of well-being.

That is not always so. Life brings changes. Changes mean inconveniences. They mean regrets. Changes mean ripping apart the sense of rightness and ease with which people fit into the world. Changes also mean opportunities for developing new internal resources and new ways of responding to life's challenges. The biggest and most difficult challenge of all is accepting change and growing from it.

What Is Loss?

Our most meaningful connections to people, things, and ideas do not always last. People grow apart. Outside events interrupt our everyday routines. New experiences affect the way people make sense of what is happening in their lives, and different ideas replace familiar ones. Death, divorce, broken friendships, and moving with the family to another city all bring losses. Broken connections to people, things, and ideas mean loss of security. When the comfortable pattern of life goes, people wonder what they can depend on now. Who or what will protect them from unknown events lying ahead? Who or what will soothe their fears or offer praise when they do something wonderful? People feel that if the people and things they had counted on to be there for them go, what is left to trust?

Losses may be clear-cut. Death and divorce rudely separate people. A move to a new location, strained friendship, serious illness, a broken leg that keeps an athlete away from sports for six weeks, an accident to a favorite pet and the veterinarian's advice to put the animal to sleep all signal important but less clear-cut losses. Having uninvited persons look through private belongings in dresser drawers, read secret diaries, or listen in on telephone conversations mean loss of privacy. Feeling let down after a special event for which one has spent months of preparation means a loss of striving. Finding that dreams of becoming a famous scientist cannot be fulfilled because of low school grades or the economic need to go to work right after high school means loss of goals. A stolen bicycle and a lost bracelet mean losses, too. Any loss represents broken connections to important things. Only the persons involved can say what is a loss to them. What is "no big deal" to one can be a major calamity to another. Loss is a very personal event.

When people experience a loss, they feel many different emotions of grief. People feel shock or surprise, not fully believing that death, divorce, or illness has really happened. They feel anger, deep sadness, confusion, and hurt. They painfully miss the lost person, object, or goal. They feel emptiness, fear, and regret. They are uncertain about how this event will change their own lives. On the other hand, they feel relief and happiness when an unpleasant situation ends. When a severely abusive parent finally leaves home or when a terminally ill and suffering relative at last gains peace through death, the loss often brings a renewing calm.

When a loss occurs, any feeling becomes possible. Someone dies. Those close to the deceased feel sadness about the parting, regret for the unkindnesses done the deceased during life, anger about the good times ahead that now will never happen. They feel confusion about what to do next, disbelief that the death has really happened, giddiness and relief that the pain suffered these last few weeks has finally ended. People experiencing loss feel depressed, resentful, or frustrated. They feel indifferent if the deceased meant nothing to them and if the death will make no change in their lives. All these feelings and more are natural and normal. They are internal cues telling the individuals what the event means to them. Feelings are neither right nor wrong. They simply are.

Feelings influence behaviors, and people experiencing loss temporarily act differently from their usual ways. People can no longer concentrate on their work. They cannot read the newspaper and absorb the meaning. They begin to focus on a task and end up daydreaming or staring blankly into space. They feel tired all the time and make careless mistakes. Their speech and movement resemble a slow-motion newsreel. Ambitious persons suddenly see their goals as meaningless, and they lose hope. They see no point in moving ahead. Their purpose fades. Appetites change, and people become extremely hungry or without any desire to eat. Some grieving people want to sleep all the time, whereas others lie tossing, unable to fall asleep.

Grieving persons sometimes alter their sexual behaviors. Some want more sexual activity than they used to have; others lose interest in any sexual behavior. Other people grieving over a loss feel angry all the time and seem ready to begin an argument at the slightest provocation. Their words bite sarcastically while their gestures seem to push people away. Still others keep busy, filling every moment with activity and not stopping until they fall into bed at night. They feel pressure to keep going and not let their feelings spill out.

These feelings and behaviors last for days, weeks, or longer depending on the person involved and on the degree of the loss. The more important the lost person or object to the individual, and the more the individual fights the strong feelings that result from the broken connection, the longer the grieving feelings and behaviors continue. Janet did not want to think about her grandmother's death. It hurt to remember how close and loving they had been, so Janet told herself that she would not dwell on the past or on her loss. She would not let herself cry over something that was over and could not be changed. She would bravely put the event behind her.

After the funeral, Janet continued school, busier than ever. Whenever she started recalling her grandmother's kindness, Janet pushed the thoughts out of her mind with more activities. Several months later, Janet's parents noticed how well their daughter was handling the death, but her girlfriends were commenting on how rude Janet was becoming. When they asked how she was, Janet met their concern with cold put-downs. She made silly mistakes in her cheering routines and then exploded in a storm of curses. She stopped going out for sodas with her friends after practice. Her school grades began dropping, and she said she was too tired to concentrate on her studies. Janet did not allow herself to feel the loss fully or to accept the meaning of her grandmother's death. The grieving behaviors continued to interrupt her life and interfere with her relationships and responsibilities.

Janet experienced an obvious loss, and she might have expected to feel strong emotions about the event. Stan's loss was less obvious. He did not know that he could feel these same emotions for a loss less overwhelming than death. Stan's father was a career Air Force officer, and the family moved to a new duty station every few years. Stan's older brother and sister had been in and out of six schools between kindergarten and high school graduation. They never became too involved with the people or activities at any stop, because they realized that they would soon move again.

Stan thought it would be different for him. His father retired from the military and accepted a civilian research position shortly before Stan entered ninth grade. Stan assumed he would be able to spend his full four years at this high school, so he became involved. He was a varsity pole vaulter, won class offices as a sophomore and junior, and had a steady girlfriend. He invested time and energy in his school and his relationships. Stan looked forward to his senior year when he would be Student Government president, athletic star, member of a popular group, and preparing for college.

One day, without warning, his father announced that he had accepted a promotion and a move to the company's headquarters in another state. The family would leave in three months. Stan listened in shocked silence. What about his friends, his sports, or his college recommendations? Was all he had done for his school and himself for nothing?

"Enough!" he told himself curtly. "Moving is part of this family's life-style and that is the end of that!" So Stan stopped thinking about what the move would mean and once again began to pack. He grew moody and uncooperative. He did not want to talk about the move with his friends and began arguing with them. He started spending more time alone. He did not want to eat as much as he used to, and he often woke up in the middle of the night to tell himself that he was a jerk for feeling so strongly about the move. Stan did not realize that a loss had occurred, so his grieving feelings seemed inappropriate. He cut them short. When he arrived at his next school, Stan went through the motions of attending classes and filling out his college applications, but he was like a zombie. He rarely talked or smiled and cared little whether he made friends. He felt the move to be totally unfair to him but told himself that he was ridiculous for making a big deal out of something he should have been expecting all along.

Although Janet and Stan had different types of losses, they both tried to ignore their feelings about the events. Janet did not want to feel the sorrowful emptiness of her lost relationship. Stan did not want to feel his resentment and sadness about an event that was typical for his family but not something he expected to create such strong emotions. Not allowing themselves to experience whatever feelings they were actually having kept the strong feelings coming and kept their behaviors confusing to themselves and annoying to others long after the loss itself had passed.

Losses are personal. Sometimes an important event creates the feelings associated with grief. At other times it is the feeling of sadness, anger, frustration, or numbness that tells the person experiencing it that a significant event has occurred. Feelings tell us what an event means to us. Feelings exist. They are neither good nor bad. We have choices about how to express those feelings once we become aware of them. Ignoring grieving feelings means that they can influence our actions in ways we seem unable to understand or control. Facing and accepting feelings means creating choices for responsible ways to act on them.

Loss: A Special Problem for Adolescents

Grieving is a difficult process for everyone, but it is a particularly trying time for adolescents.

Loss and Identity   Adolescents work at defining themselves. Through experiences with other people and activities, they learn more about who they are, what they believe, and whom they wish to become. To accomplish independence, young people look to their friends. Belonging to a group of friends means they can feel independent of their parents without having to stick their necks out too far. Secure with their friends, adolescents can laugh at their parents, put down their old-fashioned, controlling ways, and feel at ease away from home. Friends care for them as persons apart from their families. Belonging to the group gives members a feeling of well-being, importance, and confidence.

This process of separating from families and defining themselves works best when all is well at home. Young people can safely leave a stable, predictable family environment because it will not change while they go elsewhere. As much as adolescents complain about their parents never changing with the times, this consistency gives them the confidence to walk out the door and test their new independence. Adolescents need to be able to reject their parents' values and behaviors. Young people feel a sense of their own power when they can temporarily turn their backs on their families and act as free agents with their friends.

When the family begins rumbling and falling apart through separating parents, divorce, or death, the predictability is shattered. Adolescents find that when they leave home, they do not find the same conditions when they return. They cannot predict what will happen during their absence. As a result, many young people feel less confident about leaving home. They fear leaving home physically because they feel needed to smooth out arguments, offer comfort and support, and help with household tasks that keep the family together. They fear leaving home emotionally because they worry about what their parents will do next to hurt each other or their children. Even when they are outside the home, adolescents from troubled families worry about what is happening to their lives. Unstable home lives interfere with adolescents' needs to separate from their families and begin defining their own places in the world. Young people lose the confidence to try out the new attitudes and behaviors that are so essential to establishing who they are. They believe that if their parents' act so hurtfully or foolishly, perhaps the children's own judgment is also open to question. If their parents once believed they were in love but now feel only anger toward each other, maybe the young person will also be unable to hold on to a serious relationship.

For some adolescents, unstable home situations weaken the willingness to leave the family and build their own lives. It saps their confidence and good feelings about themselves. It encourages them to depend more on their friends' decisions because they do not trust their own. Without self-assurance, these persons avoid opportunities to act on their own and to build independence skills. They remain open to peer pressure because they do not trust their own opinions.

Troubled families live with a great deal of stress that hurts all involved. The members of a family in conflict cannot concentrate. Their attention span is shortened, and they cannot finish jobs they begin. Under stress, they can no longer think clearly enough to solve abstract problems, and they make poorer decisions.[1] Adolescents in these families feel nervous and jumpy much of the time. They cannot learn, and schoolwork becomes meaningless exercises. They cannot finish homework or plan how to begin

---

[1] Beal, Edward, "Separation, Divorce, and Single Parent Families," Carter, E. A., and McGoldrick, M., eds., *The Family Life Cycle: A Framework for Family Therapy* (New York: Gardner Press, 1980): 246.

major assignments. They feel depressed and tired and experience many physical ailments. They develop problems
with their friends. Some stressed adolescents become lon-
ers. Some become very involved with their unhappy parents, acting as confidants as they listen to their parents'
complaints. Others assume so much responsibility for
household chores that they become almost servants. Some
young people cling to their friends, accepting all group
decisions, even those with which they might normally disagree. Anxious young people often become eager to please
their friends and hold on to their peer relationships even at
the cost of their own values, goals, and sense of who they
are as individuals. Unstable families threaten adolescents'
evolving identities.

Not all adolescents, however, have serious problems with
loss. Those who have already started separating emotionally from their families and have developed confidence in
their own abilities go on without serious problems. Naturally, they feel sad about the death or divorce, but they do
not allow the loss to shake their confidence. These young
people view their parents as regular people, not as powerful agents against whom to rebel or upon whom to rely
totally. For these adolescents, loss means assuming even
more responsibility sooner for leading their own lives. They
are now in charge of their schoolwork and home chores.
They carry out their commitments well. They make sound
decisions. Moreover, they do not depend so much on their
friends' version of how to behave. Although belonging to
a group gives them support during trying times at home,
these adolescents do not desperately need their friends' approval in order to feel good about themselves. They know
that they already have the skills to make a successful ad-
justment to the loss and effectively master their own lives.

Loss and Feelings Loss creates particularly difficult problems for adolescents because it brings strong emotions. The anger, confusion, sadness, and fear that come with loss of an important relationship or goal greatly disturb young people. Frightening new emotions seem to arise from nowhere and hit with a forceful wallop. Young people seeking to become the masters of their own lives suddenly feel helpless. They do not always recognize or understand these feelings, and the force and changeability of their emotions make young people feel embarrassed, guilty, or afraid. Without awareness of how to face and spend these emotions, naive adolescents remain at their mercy. As a result, they feel like small, scared children, and their self-confidence weakens still more.

Adolescents also have difficulty understanding and accepting their unclear and illogical feelings. Although they experience unpleasant emotions, many young people do not realize that a loss has occurred. Being cut from a team, not receiving a bid to join a popular club, moving to a new city, finishing a semester-long science project, or breaking up with a close friend do not seem like major tragedies. They do, however, represent major losses, and the grief feels just as real and sharp as if a dear relative had died. "Minor" troubles look like small concerns to outsiders, but only those who are directly involved can honestly say whether or not the loss was a big one. Adolescents need permission to accept their losses as important enough to feel sorry, depressed, or angry about, no matter how petty they appear to a casual onlooker.

In addition, adolescents do not realize that they can both love and hate their parents. Young people often feel two different emotions about the same person. They may truly love a father for his past thoughtfulness and support but at the same time bitterly resent the way he now treats their mother, his wife. Adolescents may adore a single, working mother for her willingness to spend time listening to their troubles while feeling deeply angry about the way she gives her eldest child too many cooking, cleaning, and baby-sitting chores. Hating another person's behavior does not make adolescents ungrateful children. Disliking a parent's attitudes or actions does not take away from the genuine love felt for that parent at other times. Loving is not an all-or-nothing emotion. Relationships are not built on either-or feelings. Feelings depend on the long-term relationship as well as on current behaviors. Individuals can experience both loving and hating feelings toward others without being considered terrible people. People feel what they truly feel. In times of conflict, people naturally have conflicting emotions.

Likewise, adolescents have difficulty understanding that all relationships exist separate from each other. Feelings toward one person do not take away from or cancel out feelings toward another. They can love their friends and also love their parents. They can become especially close to certain teachers without feeling any less affection for their fathers and mothers. In the same way, young people can feel appreciation and love toward individuals whom their own divorced parents have recently married without being disloyal or uncaring toward their real divorced or deceased parents. People cannot compete for a person's love. Buying presents and spending time with persons must be activities freely given for the pleasure of sharing company without thinking about how many positive emotions these are worth at cash-in time.

Adolescents feel obligations toward their real parents. Young people sometimes suspect that liking their steppar-ents marks them as traitors. No one outside the relationship can break strong emotional ties to natural parents. No person can replace another, and no two relationships are exactly alike. Adolescents can love both natural parents and stepparents without feeling that they are taking affection away from one in order to give it to the other. When it comes to giving love, there is more than enough to go around.

Strong feelings also stem from unfinished situations. Adolescents do not always have or make the opportunity to say "goodbye" to dying loved ones. They cannot always ask forgiveness for all the little rudenesses they gave the other while they were together. They have not told the other how much they appreciated the kindnesses and how happy they felt when together. For many in our society, showing loving feelings signals weakness, and they regard a silent acceptance of pain or love as a sign of maturity. This belief works against people's openly and directly expressing their true feelings to others when it can make the most difference in their relationship. This belief also leads adolescents to suffer much silent guilt about their own conflicts or thoughtlessness with the lost person.

Similarly, young people do not always have or make the opportunity to tell divorcing parents how angry and unhappy the fighting adults make their children while the marriage falls apart. Young people do not easily express their resentment or fondness for those who influenced the growth of those feelings. So when the relationship suddenly changes through death, divorce, or a broken romance, the unspoken emotions remain inside. Adolescents feel enormous tensions pressing to be let out, like the heavy weight shuttling back and forth on top of a hot pressure cooker. The more and stronger the unexpressed feelings, the greater is the pressure building inside.

What happens to these unspoken emotions? Where does

the rising inner tension go? Feelings turn into actions. The type of behaviors depends on how tuned-in the young people are to their own feelings. If they remain open to their emotions, they can catch the tension and track it back to its source. They wait out the queasiness and recognize the uncomfortable tension for the anger or sadness or love it represents. They can then think about how best to express the emotions constructively. These young people show confidence in their ability to endure the tension while looking for its cause. They show mature responsibility as they decide how to spend the feelings safely and appropriately.

On the other hand, young people without this confidence in themselves cannot stand the internal pressure from these unexpressed feelings. They need to get rid of the tension as quickly as possible. Not acting makes them jittery, so they behave impulsively. They strike out aggressively with fists or words to spend the tension. They always look for a fight and usually find one. Others behave in ways to dull the tension temporarily by using drugs or by distracting themselves with adventurous excitement.

The unconfident young people hurt themselves in two ways. First, they never learn what truly bothers them, and thus cannot really solve their problems. At best, they can find only short-term diversions. Second, these adolescents become very open to peer pressure. Without trust in themselves and without an important sustaining relationship elsewhere, they depend heavily on peer opinion for direction and support. They willingly go along with their friends' outrageous plans for entertainment. The wilder the time, the less chance to feel the inner pressures. Stress weakens their problem-solving ability. They cannot look ahead and anticipate difficulties, so they make poor decisions. Such dangerous behaviors often cause more problems than the adolescents had in the first place. Nevertheless, these young people need their friends' acceptance as reassurance that they are still worthwhile persons. Friends' approval reassures them that people still care for them.

Types of Loss During Adolescence

Broken Romance   Adolescents gain much from their relationships. Friends provide a sense of identity and importance for young people trying to define themselves. Boygirl relationships particularly mean a lot, because pairing marks an adult behavior. Becoming part of a couple brings peers' respect and admiration. Romances give young people chances to feel and express new intense emotions. Within these relationships, they also start learning how to deal with love, affection, sharing, and sexual attraction. Romance is a special, exciting experience.

What is more, romances provide occasions for adolescents to learn to deal with misunderstandings and hurt feelings. People sometimes do things that the other dislikes. They say things that the other resents. Young people begin developing intimacy skills and do not always understand what the other persons' words or actions mean. Does Jerry's desire to visit a friend Saturday afternoon without his girlfriend at his side mean that he no longer cares for her? When Carolyn tells Al that she wants to continue dating other boys in addition to him, does it mean that she does not take the relationship with him seriously? When Tom tells Shirley that he does not want her to discuss her family's problems with him, does Tom mean that he does not like her enough? Young people find it difficult to know the truth of a situation. Yet with issues of identity and selfworth tightly wrapped up in these relationships, the answers matter a great deal.

Young people have difficulty recognizing and accepting

when relationships end. They approach relationships from an either-or, all-or-nothing perspective. They either care deeply for another person or they could not care less. If they truly like another, they cannot like or show awareness of any person outside the relationship without being disloyal. If once important relationships end, adolescents believe that suddenly all the value becomes worthless. For them, endings cancel out all prior satisfactions and good times. If the pair is kaput, then their own value and importance as individuals also end.

Adolescents believe the myths of eternal love and friendship. As a result, they do not expect their relationships to change and cannot accept the changes that naturally occur. With shared experiences, couples grow closer together or find they actually have little in common. Believing in "happily every after," adolescents fear change in relationships because they do not expect it. When things do change, they do not want to accept the differences.

Bonnie, age fifteen, met Frank at a roller-skating party. He was the same age, and they seemed to enjoy each other's company. During the following month they saw a lot of each other. Skating, movies, and telephone calls kept them in contact. Frank was the first young man to show serious interest in Bonnie, and her head spun. She felt special and prized.

During the fifth week Frank called only once. The next week he phoned to say that he was going out of town to visit relatives. On a date after that, Bonnie returned from the Ladies' Room to find Frank talking with another girl. Bonnie felt confused and hurt, but she did not mention it to Frank. The next week, he did not call her once. When Bonnie did see him at the skating rink, he smiled broadly at her and then looked away. His coolness frightened her, but she forced herself to speak with him.

"Don't you want to see me anymore?'' she half-joked. "No!'' answered Frank and then turned the conversation in a different direction.

Bonnie, hurt, asked herself what she had done wrong. Why didn't Frank like her anymore? What could she do to win him back? Over and over, she asked herself what had happened. She became more and more depressed. She could think of nothing but Frank. While her teachers lectured, she wrote his name in her notebook. She drew his initials instead of completing her assignments. With friends, she constantly talked about Frank and their troubles.

Six months later, Bonnie had lost weight, earned poor school grades, had dark circles under her eyes, and still spoke sadly about Frank. She could not let go. She did not understand what had happened and kept hammering at the "why's'' to no avail. Bonnie did not expect the relationship to change. When it did, she refused to accept that it was over. To her, Frank was still her boyfriend but they were having difficult times.

Adolescents have many ways of handling broken romances. These relationships mean so much that few permit them to end once they are over. Young people find unusual ways to hold on to the relationships even after the couple no longer go together.

Many, like Bonnie, hold on by suffering. Suffering proves their enduring love. They feel depressed, lose appetite and the ability to concentrate. They become unkempt and sad all the time. With the other person gone, playing the martyr allows them to keep the relationship alive in their minds and in their actions. In this way, the lost person remains part of their daily experience, if only in sad thoughts.

In addition, sufferers continue feeling sad in order to prove the worth of their original emotions for the person from whom they are now separated. When the relationship worked, the participants felt sincere and genuine affection for their partner. When the relationship ends they ask if their first feelings were real. "How can people feel love one day and feel nothing the next?" they ask. Did they really feel those feelings or was it all a dream? Continuing to suffer long after the relationship ends allows the sufferer to say, "See how genuine my feelings were! I loved so much that the feelings still remain with me."

In another way of handling broken romances, adolescents feel constant outrage toward the other person for treating them so badly. Although the injustice may have occurred weeks before, the young persons daily feel fresh anger about the breakup. As with sorrow, anger helps keep the lost relationship a current event through active emotions that focus on it. Although physically elsewhere, the separated other becomes tied to them in thoughts and through continually renewed angry feelings.

Many times, young people hold on to a finished romance through anger directed at themselves. "How could I have been so stupid!" "How could I have acted so foolishly!" Regrets turn into chances to kick themselves for making mistakes during the relationship. These adolescents blame themselves totally for the breakup. They cannot forgive themselves for natural misunderstandings or for changes in the other person over which they had no control.

Young people handle broken romances in a different way when they cover up their feelings. They deny their original loving feelings and their present emptiness. "It does not matter." "It's not a big deal!" "That's life!" they explain as concerned friends ask about the split. If the adolescents can prove to themselves and to others that they feel no important loss after the split, they can convince themselves that nothing important occurred. Nothing of value lost means they did not risk all in a doomed relationship. In this way, they save face and keep their friends' respect. They believe that they stand above disappointment or regret. They want to believe that they cannot be touched by another's actions. They want to feel no loss now so they can tell themselves that they still have worth. No hurt feelings mean no loss has occurred. No loss means no failure.

In addition, many adolescents idealize the person from whom they are separated. The lost other becomes the best, the sweetest, the kindest, and the most thoughtful person in the world. The person takes on super-special characteristics that no ordinary person can duplicate. The relationship may be over, but no replacement is possible. The loss creates such unrealistic expectations for future relationships that no mortal stands a chance. The ended romance becomes the last in which the person becomes involved. No more romances means no more hurt and no more loss.

Adolescents use these loss strategies to ease their pain. An important relationship brings strong pleasant emotions, a sense of who they are, and their friends' respect. Its loss means an overwhelming disappointment. The loss threatens their good feelings about themselves. It confuses the recently settled issues of who they are, what is their value, and where they are going. Young people hold on to sad and angry feelings about the other person and themselves, deny that they are disappointed, or idealize the other person to protect themselves. Strong feelings keep them emotionally tied to the other person even though the individual is no longer physically present. They maintain an invisible relationship and feel as if they are not really alone. Holding on to lost relationships also keeps the persons from becoming involved in new romances. With their emotions still safely invested in the first romance, they are not free to enter into a new one. They do not again have to risk disappointment or loneliness. If they suffer the loss or keep the anger, at least those emotions feel familiar. They cannot then be engulfed in sudden new feelings that might devastate them completely.

What is more, young people's tendency to approach life with an all-or-nothing philosophy mistakenly makes them think that if a relationship ends, it was worthless from the start. They suspect that all the good feelings and enjoyable times they shared were complete lies. In relationships, however, the ends do not necessarily give meaning to all that went before. The couple did share deep and important feelings. They did learn to understand how another person viewed the world. They did have many memorable times together. They experienced real and special feelings even though the relationship did not last. The relationship was as genuine and meaningful as the participants made it. If one or both were not willing or able to make the relationship more than it turned out to be, that does not necessarily reflect evil intent. Young people continue learning about themselves and about others. Relationships often serve this end. When young people achieve more maturity, they will be able to achieve greater and longer-lasting intimacy in their relationships. Entering, enjoying, and ending romances make up part of the process. For adolescents, getting involved is important. Feeling their emotions and discovering what they mean is important. When young people can end a romance and ask, "What do I feel now?" and "What have I learned about myself and others from this experience?" they grow more able to develop deeper, more meaningful relationships in the future.

Peer pressure affects adolescents' romances in several ways. First, friends place much importance on dating and being popular with members of the opposite sex. They admire and respect group members who can be part of a couple. This expectation creates pressure to become or remain part of a pair. Needing the romance to keep face with the group, many young people get involved in relationships with others for whom they do not deeply care. Lack of strong emotional ties in the pair makes honest communication difficult. When misunderstandings occur, the parties do not know or care enough to work them out. Frequent arguments and breakups result. This serves as a fruitful conversation topic in the group, securing as much importance in the rehashing as it did in the pairing.

Next, since romances carry so much value to the peer group, members are often reluctant to let go of faltering, meaningless, or ended relationships. The suffering, anger, and idealizing that prevent individuals from letting go also allow them to save face with the group. In these ways they still remain part of a couple even though the couple presently spend their time apart.

Lastly, broken romances weaken individuals' self-confidence and sense of who they are. Without their romantic partner, they feel less important than before. They feel less competent and assured because the breakup seems like a personal failure. These attitudes make peer pressure a stronger influence in their lives. They now need their friends' approval and acceptance more than ever. They trust their friends' opinions because the breakup shook confidence in their own. They become more likely to go along with the group in order to feel accepted and appreciated once more.

Divorce and Remarriage   Divorce and its aftermath do not always bring special problems for adolescents. Those young people who have already separated emotionally from their parents and are able to view them as ''just folks'' find these times inconvenient and unpleasant but not tragic. These mature adolescents know themselves, their worth as individuals, and where they are going. Their battling parents may argue with each other, yet the children can step safely outside the combat. They understand that their parents divorce, not they.

Nevertheless, divorce unsettles the household and upsets the adolescents' process of developing their own identities. Young people need to separate from their families and discover their own unique personalities. They must push away many of their parents' values and behaviors and try on new ways of being themselves. Every time young people can shut the door on their parents' ways and successfully carry out new approaches to problem solving, they build confidence in their abilities to take charge of their lives. Whenever they use their parents' approaches to problem-solving independent of their elders, they also gain confidence in their own abilities. When their parents' marriage ties begin to unravel and the home situation becomes unstable, however, young people feel less willing to leave home emotionally or physically. They fear that if they spend time in outside activities, they risk having no family left to which to return.

On the other hand, when new stepfamilies come together, the newly married adults often want to build a close-knit feeling among the new family members. They plan activities to foster this spirit of we-ness. Unfortunately, this plan runs against their adolescents' desires to spend more time outside the family. What adults consider important at this time represents just the opposite of what their adolescents think important. This conflict brings grounds for new arguments at home.

Not wanting to feel dependent on their parents yet being unwilling to leave the disturbing situation at home for outside interests puts young people on the spot. They do not want to stay, and they do not want to leave. They desperately want to make the troubled situation better, but they do not know how. A helpless, frightened feeling results. Instead of becoming increasingly mature and self-sufficient, young people of divorce become more and more frantic and tied to their families. These no-win events undermine their confidence in their own ability, judgment, and value. As a result, when with their friends, these stressed adolescents show impaired problem-solving skills, reduced capacity to concentrate, and lower self-confidence, and they become open to peer pressure.

Not only do these young people come to their friends with fewer personal resources, but they are more in need of the group's continued support and affection. Battling parents do not usually make time to hear their adolescents' concerns; they have enough trouble keeping their own lives on course. Without reassurance from their parents, young people rely more on their friends' ongoing interest and approval. This, too, leads to adolescents' increased willingness to go along blindly with their friends' ideas.

While their youth and inexperience create problems for developing their ideas about who they are, their age also puts adolescents into a special position at home. Physically, many adolescents look like adults. Emotionally, they show perceptiveness and deep understanding of other people's pressures and circumstances. In turn, parents view these near-adults as people with whom to share their troubles. Adolescents become their unhappy parents' confidants, protectors, and go-betweens. More mature than their younger brothers and sisters, adolescents find themselves hearing more than they want to know about their mothers' unfaithfulness or their fathers' crudeness. Flattered on one hand by their parents' respect for their opinions, adolescents also feel guilt about their inability to solve their parents' difficulties and keep the family together. Moreover, adolescents feel strong resentment that one loved parent would bitterly attack the other in front of them.

At these times, parents place young people in an impossible position. Adolescents cannot choose one parent over another. Regardless of how cruelly adults treat each other, adolescents can cherish and show loyalty to them both. If parents force a loyalty test, the young people cannot win. They feel only confusion and sadness about the parent not picked. This situation further weakens adolescents' self-confidence and makes them easier targets for peer pressure.

Additionally, the avalanche of feelings stemming from life in a conflict-ridden family makes adolescents more open to peer influence. These adolescents feel guilt because they suspect they may have caused the family problems in the first place. At the very least, they did nothing to prevent the breakup. They feel anger toward one or both battling parents for tearing the family apart or for not practicing what they preach about the values of family unity. Similarly, adolescents feel guilty about "hating" someone they love. They feel helpless to remedy the situation. Nothing they try to do seems to make the family stronger or make the parents love each other again. Adolescents feel confused and torn when parents demand that they choose sides in the adults' arguments. Young people secretly feel afraid that parents who once told the world how much in love they were may one day stop loving their children, too. Adolescents fear that they may have inherited their parents' faults and tendency toward having bad relationships. They feel distrustful of everything. They distrust their own relationships with others, their abilities to predict and master events in their own lives, and their views of themselves as valuable, capable persons. They feel depressed, overwhelmingly sad and tired, full of doubts, and without hope. The whole affair leaves them emotionally drained, unable to work on building their own lives.

Finally, separation, divorce, and remarriage raise questions about adolescents' sexual identity. Young people hear their parents argue about lack of affection and marital infidelities before the divorce. Many adolescents therefore assume that sexual problems caused their parents' split. Once the parents live in separate households, adolescents frequently see unfamiliar men and women coming to date their newly single parents. Sexual attitudes and behaviors kept private in most families become public events in single-parent homes as the parents prepare to see other adults socially. Parents dress up for dates, act nervous and silly while waiting to go out, and often expect more from their dates than a goodnight kiss. They show the same behaviors that their adolescent children do in their own romances.

Young people beginning to ask who they are as sexual persons find their parents' dating to be awkward and upsetting. "This is what young persons are supposed to do," they think. "Adults have no right to act this way." Not used to viewing their mothers and fathers as sexual persons, adolescents become uncomfortable with the idea of sex.

Adolescents of divorcing or separated parents wonder about their own beliefs regarding proper sexual attitudes and behaviors for themselves. They feel confused about the role of sex in their lives. Some react disgustedly to sex, silently saying, "See what terrible things happen when you become sexually active!" These young people decide that they want nothing to do with such powerful and destructive behaviors. They refuse to date seriously or to act in sexual ways.

Others feel anger toward their parents' inability to keep the family together and judge sexual problems to be their parents' major failing. These adolescents think, "Sex is the most important part of a relationship, and Mom and Dad messed it up. I can get and keep a man or woman better than they could!" As a result, these young people become flirtatious and involved in many sexual affairs. They try to prove to themselves that they do not have to be afraid of losing a relationship because of sex. Especially when the newly single parents begin dating, adolescent children often feel anger and fear. They act out these emotions by openly competing with their sexually active parents.

Young people try to make their shattered world safer by building ties to others. They use sex as a way to secure those ties. Through sexual activity, these young people try to reassure themselves that they will not fail in the same ways they suspect that their parents failed. With sexual behaviors, adolescents gain attention, affection, and closeness that help them feel like important people again. Shaken by the divorce, through sex they feel that someone still loves them. They can also express their anger toward their parents by going the grown-ups one better in the same area where their parents feel the least secure—their ability to have intimate relationships.

Living in stepfamilies creates still more frustrations. The wife arrives with children from her first marriage while the husband arrives with his. Blending these two families sometimes brings increased sexual tensions into the household. Stepparents now live in the same home as their mate's attractive, almost-adult adolescents. Female adolescents live one room away from male adolescents who are not really their brothers. Physical attraction, physical closeness, and limited privacy in such blended families at times make opportunities for sexual involvement among more than the recently wedded couple. While the incest taboos against sexual involvement with blood relatives remain clear, the rules governing sexual relations among members of blended families are not.

When young people express confusion about their own sexual values and attitudes, they try out different sexual behaviors in the real world and ask, "Is this me? Am I comfortable with myself when I act this way?" If they answer "No," they can stop the behavior. They have learned more about themselves from the experience even if they decide not to repeat it. When these adolescents also question their own sense of personal worth, importance, and ability to act as independent adults, however, they become more willing to act in ways that their friends think appropriate, whether or not the behaviors fit them as individuals. Separation, divorce, and remarriage raise serious questions and doubts about themselves in adolescents' minds. Whatever takes away from their sense of competence and value as individuals makes peer pressure a greater influence in their lives. At these times, adolescents become more willing to say "Okay" to their friends' suggestions about sexual activities than they usually would be. Through sex, young people can act out their anger, fear, and confusion. They can gain temporary reassurance, affection, and tenderness. In addition, their adultlike actions in sexual areas can earn their friends' respect and admiration.

Adolescent Suicide Loss means a difficult experience for adolescents. Never before have they felt so close to other people. Never before have they had such a range of deep and complex feelings. Never before have they directly faced an important event without a protective adult filtering its impact. Just as young people gain an awareness of life's possibilities, open themselves to an ongoing future, and further develop their skills for taking charge of their own lives, reality stuns them with the fact that there are no guarantees. No promises exist that all the hard work will amount to anything. No matter how talented the individual, life remains unpredictable. No matter how strongly one loves another person, relationships do not last forever. Plans go awry. People are imperfect. Relationships change. People die.

Young people suffer loss with many feelings and thoughts. At first they feel shock and disbelief. They cannot believe that the tragic event really happened. With all their hearts, they do not want it to be true. Maybe, they bargain, if they act more considerately at home or earn better grades at school, the event will not be true. Perhaps if the young persons act as if they will completely fall apart, the event will reverse itself and everything will be as it was before.

Then the depression comes. Depression brings lack of sleep or loss of appetite. Adolescents feel tired all the time and don't have the energy or interest to care about anything. They seem sad and slow-moving, unable to concentrate on schoolwork. They stop spending time with friends, preferring, instead, to be alone. They feel unhappy alone, too. Many develop backaches, headaches, stomachaches, rashes, or nervous mannerisms. They stop caring about how they look or what they do. Some depressed young people, however, show no outward signs of depression even though they think, "So what! It's all hopeless anyway!"

For most adolescents the depression eventually passes, and they begin to accept the sad event. They feel sad that it happened, and they can never forget the lost person or idea, but they begin looking ahead once more, pick up their lives, and move on. For many others, unable to get out from under the draining depression, suicide becomes a possible way out.

The suicide rate among young people ages fifteen to nineteen has tripled since 1955. Thirteen adolescents a day kill themselves. For every suicide completed, fifty people attempt to kill themselves.[2] Adolescents suffering depression after a severe loss cannot think clearly. Many have not slept well for a long time. Their energy and perspective go. As a result, they cannot solve their problems. They feel themselves falling further and further behind. Nothing matters. They see no way out. These young people do not really want to be dead, but they do want their lives as they are to stop. Along with depression, mood swings, self-doubts, and the lack of problem-solving skills make matters worse.

Many situations lead to adolescent suicide. Young people from divorced families or with two parents dedicated to building their own careers often feel totally alone, as if they do not belong anywhere or to anyone.[3] Feelings of being alone in a threatening world lead to thoughts of suicide. Taking drugs such as LSD occasionally causes the users to imagine that they see or hear things not actually there. They might respond to their hallucination by accidentally or intentionally killing themselves. Other very angry young people view suicide as a way to hurt their indifferent parents or friends. They imagine that attempted or actual suicide will force the survivors to feel guilty about how poorly they had treated the victim. For others, suicide represents an impulsive response to a strong disappointment. Angry about the turn of events, young people believe for the moment that their lives are not worth living.

Some adolescents closely follow the careers of TV and

[2] "Teen-Age Suicide," *Newsweek* (August 28, 1978): 74.
[3] Op cit.

recording stars who they feel are like themselves. If the celebrity commits suicide, the young persons who closely identify with the important individual may be prompted to do the same thing. Another group, young people fighting to earn top grades in school in order to enter prestigious universities or win important jobs after graduation, often feel tremendous pressure to perform well. Fear of slipping and losing everything sometimes leads these intelligent young people to thoughts of suicide. Finally, young people who know or suspect that they may be dying of a fatal disease or those who have had a serious physical injury that threatens to change their life-style dramatically consider killing themselves.

When adolescents experience great stress, feel their lives not worth living, and lack the self-confidence to wait until the pain passes before making any important decisions about what to do next, suicide becomes a possibility. When these unhappy persons cut themselves off from their friends or close relatives and no longer stay in active contact with those who mean the most to them, suicide becomes a still greater risk. For suicidal adolescents, remaining an active member of a peer group helps provide emotional support during the most difficult times. Friends bring warmth, caring, and choices about how to solve problems. Friends tell grieving or angry adolescents that although this may be a terrible time for them, they are not alone.

If peer support does not give grieving young people hope for better times ahead, friends' sensitivity to each other at least makes them able to notice behavior signs that suggest a potential suicide. Although would-be suicides frequently appear to parents and outsiders to be well adjusted and in control, most people who kill themselves give verbal or behavioral warnings, openly or secretly, of their plan. Su-

icidal adolescents are more likely to discuss their problems
and thoughts with their friends than with their parents. In
fact, lack of a close relationship with parents contributes
to suicide.[4]

Warning signs come in many forms. For instance, if the
young persons have tried to kill themselves before, they
may respond to the current loss of hope by attempting suicide again. The despairing adolescents may get the means
for killing themselves by buying pills or a gun or by hiding
a knife or rope in their bedrooms. Desperate adolescents
sometimes talk or write about their desire to end their lives
and reveal their sense of total failure. Some give away
their most valued possessions to close friends or write a
suicide note.

They may have recently lost a loved one through death
or divorce. They feel separated from important family
members, dear friends, or favorite pets. Potential suicides
often show sudden changes in behavior. They may have
begun staying by themselves a great deal, remaining apart
from friends who could help them over the crisis. Further
signs include changes in eating and sleeping patterns.
Young people start complaining about not getting enough
sleep or sleeping much more than they used to. School
grades drop as the young people no longer have the energy, interest, or ability to pay attention in class. These
individuals may have acted in violent or destructive ways
in the past, may have misused drugs, driven recklessly, or
run away from home.

Finally, potential suicides could be persons who have
been miserably unhappy for a long time but who suddenly

[4] Frederick, Calvin J., "Adolescent Suicide," *Advocacy for Children* (U.S. Department of HEW, Office of Human Development Services for Children, Youth, and Families, Children's Bureau, National Center for Child Advocacy), Fall 1978, p. 3.

seem relaxed and at peace once more. These individuals may have decided to kill themselves and feel relief on finding an answer to their problems.

These examples do not cover all the possible warning signs for suicidal young people. One way for friends to know if their peers are actually thinking about suicide is to ask them. Mentioning suicide does not put "crazy ideas" into the head of an adolescent who feels hopeless. Instead, directly facing the issue tells the troubled friend that someone cares enough to ask the difficult questions and offer help in solving problems. This provides a chance for the troubled young person to open up and discuss the situation.

If friends suspect a young person is considering suicide, they can help prevent the tragedy by thoughtful action. First, they should listen and try to understand the problems stressing their friend. Take seriously and calmly what the person says. The problem may not seem like a big deal to the listener, but it means a major crisis for the speaker. Ask directly whether the friend has thoughts about suicide and encourage the individual to talk or cry about the problems. Be a good friend and let the other person have the chance to talk, weep, or yell about the troubling situation. Look for evidence of the person's plan to commit suicide.

If, after the discussion, suicide seems a possibility, get help. Encourage the despairing person to talk with a parent, guidance counselor, minister, hot-line worker, older brother or sister, favorite relative, or mental health center professional. Outside, objective people often find answers that those who are closely involved miss. If the suicidal person refuses help, tell someone close to the person, such as a parent, relative, or teacher, about the situation so that they can offer support and supervision during the crisis.

The influence young people have over each other often

receives blame for a good deal of adolescent behavior. When parents and adults observe their adolescents acting in disturbing ways, they quickly blame peer pressure. When it comes to the most vivid violence against oneself, however, peer influence can save lives.

Role of Friends in Romantic Breakup

Positive peer pressure can help teens with many types of loss. When a romance goes sour, both boy and girl feel hurt and angry. Believing they had a special relationship, they now feel betrayed, disappointed, embarrassed, lonely, distrustful, and confused. They may experience many other emotions as well. All these emotions are natural responses to the loss of an important bond.

Some teens, however, want to turn a broken relationship into a soap opera. They talk about it endlessly. They mope around and stop trying to look their best. They stop living in the present because they are too busy complaining and moaning about what happened in the past.

Good friends feel sorry for a friend who has had such a big disappointment and hurt. They know their friend is having a tough time. Talking for a while about the disappointment can help put it into the past. Friends want to support each other through difficult times, and they are ready and eager to listen.

But after a few weeks of retelling the events that led to the breakup, the tales start sounding like rehashing and whining. The sad stories become boring as they are told over and over. Good friends want to help, but they are becoming sick and tired of hearing the same sad story. They see their friend holding onto the loss and living in the past instead of moving beyond it.

After an important loss, disappointment is expected.

Sadness and loneliness are typical. Wishing the situation had ended better is understandable. But preoccupation with the breakup is neither interesting nor healthy. Good friends can influence their endlessly grieving peer to stop holding on to the loss.

Positive peer pressure here says, "We care for you and feel sorry you have had such a painful experience, but the relationship and the breakup are over. Talking about it time again and again is just making you unhappy and keeping you locked in the past. Take what good you can from the experience. The relationship had some good parts even though it ended. We are your friends, and we think you are ready to get on with your life. If there's nothing more you can do about it, then you must let it go. If you really need to keep looking at the experience, maybe you should talk to a professional who could help you get over it better than we can."

Most friends think these thoughts but may not say them because they don't want to hurt their upset friend even more. They think that saying enough is enough might seem like another rejection. The question is one of how long. How long has the unhappy friend been recounting the loss of a short-term relationship? Two weeks is normal. Two months is dragging it out. If the relationship had been one of long standing, perhaps six months or longer, the loss experience will also be longer.

For positive peer pressure to help friends move beyond loss and resume living in the present, friends must be willing to let the unhappy friend express feelings of loss for a while. But when the stories are repeated and repeated without any sign of the friend pulling himself or herself together, a caring word can convey two messages to the griever. One, continued retelling is not going to win additional support from friends. Second, the unhappy friend needs a referral to a mental health professional who can really help him or her to move beyond the loss and back into the present. Either message may be the best help yet for the endless griever.

Conclusion

Loss hurts. Just as young people are gaining confidence in their ability to master their own lives as independent individuals, change occurs. A person dies. A family divorces. A severe injury, a move to a new location, or a dream suddenly given up as impractical means broken connections. The rules change drastically even as the players are learning the game.

Many events bring loss, and loss brings a wide range of emotions. Coping with change in one's life is difficult. Coping with the feelings and behaviors resulting from that change is difficult. The whole experience raises new questions for adolescents about who they are and where they're going. Young people can respond to this challenge by assuming greater responsibility for themselves sooner, by losing self-confidence and relying more heavily on their friends' options, or by questioning their own value and worthiness to continue living.

Grief lasts well beyond the actual loss—much longer unless it is faced, felt, and accepted. Young people can cope with loss by letting themselves feel their emotions whether or not they seem logical to outsiders. They can decide how to express them appropriately, and they can help their friends do the same.

Chapter **VI**

Peer Pressure and Special Populations

All young people share common goals. They want to understand themselves better and find their place in the world. They want skills and reassurance that they can handle themselves effectively away from their parents' control. They want to be like others and feel accepted. In addition, most young people want the chance to know and act on their own opinions when they are making important decisions.

Everyone differs in some ways and shares similarities in others. Finding areas of uniqueness becomes one of adolescents' major jobs. Many individuals, however, learn that they differ from their age-mates long before they reach their teens. Gifted children, learning-disabled children, and children of ethnic and racial minorities discover their differentness either before first attending school or shortly after. While classmates are studying their lessons and just being kids, these special youngsters become aware of their differentness. They face their separateness earlier than do their peers because they possess certain qualities of intelligence, learning style, or family background that vividly set them apart. As a result, these special young people soon confront peer pressure.

Gifted Adolescents and Peer Pressure

Gifted individuals differ from their age-mates in several ways. They have above average ability in academic skills. They read and understand assignments quickly. They write the most in-depth reports, build the most complicated projects, and ask the most penetrating questions. Gifted individuals enjoy solving problems and following their curiosity wherever it leads. Enthusiastic learners, they have energy to spare. Frequently their solutions show great imagination and originality. Gifted young people have confidence in their abilities because they have been successful using them. Independent, questioning persons, they challenge their parents and teachers with "What if?" and "Why not?". They show sensitivity to their own wishes and feelings as well as to the world around them.

Gifted youngsters compose 3 to 5 percent of the students in school.[1] Few in number, they quickly stand out and receive special attention. In elementary grades, teachers ask them to write their math homework on the blackboard so all can see the "right way" to solve the problems. Teachers read their essays aloud to the class as the example of "the best" papers. Gifted persons have their hands still raised after their classmates have tried unsuccessfully to answer the teacher's question.

Outstanding school abilities in reading, math, complex thinking, and high achievement in subject areas, leadership, or the arts bring these young people much notice. Before they can be formally tested, their natural talents mark them as smart. Testing only confirms this. "Gifted" students now have a label that makes them feel even more separate from others.

[1] Martinson, Ruth A., *The Identification of the Gifted and Talented* (Office of the Ventura County Superintendent of Schools, Ventura, California), June, 1974, p. 6.

Very often, gifted youngsters, teachers, and parents do not understand what this label means. The "gifted" title confuses them and clouds the way they see themselves. Does "gifted" mean they are more intelligent than their friends? Does this make them better than their friends? Does "above average" ability mean they are not "normal"? Does having a lot of skill mean they have to do or accomplish certain things? What does their "giftedness" mean for their future school achievement, their friendships, and their later careers? Unless they can accurately understand the real meaning of giftedness, the high ability may not seem like a gift at all. Misunderstood, giftedness seems more like a penalty.

Understanding Giftedness   Gifted young people see themselves separated from their friends by teachers' expectations, parents' comments, and test scores. The fuss both pleases and upsets them. They like special praise but resent the pressure to perform, and they dislike the growing gap between themselves and their less academically successful friends. Understanding themselves becomes a task that gifted youths face years earlier than their classmates do because their uniqueness comes to the surface sooner.

Gifted young people differ from their classmates in the ways they learn and in the ways they use that learning. They can learn information faster than their peers. They read the information once, think about its meaning, and understand it. Grasping more complex information in high school or college takes longer, but their effectiveness as superior students remains. Gifted young people may learn all types of information quickly, or they may excel in a few areas. For instance, many gifted young people stand out in all studies requiring reading and complex thinking whereas others perform highly in either math or literature. Gifted individuals learn more deeply than do their peers. These special persons easily relate bits of information, see connections, form relationships, and build concepts about the way ideas fit together. Those interested in literature can recognize a play as a product of a specific historical period as well as having essential meaning true to other times and places. *King Lear,* for example, becomes not simply a 400-year-old relic but a vehicle in which leaders question the influence of political power on human relationships. Politicians today ask the same questions as do the play's characters. To other gifted students, math becomes a language used to describe physical relationships rather than a series of time-consuming homework problems.

Moreover, gifted individuals enjoy manipulating information in complex ways. They ask, "What would happen if . . . ?" attempting to push their understanding further. They find pleasure in taking aspects of information apart and reorganizing and reassembling it in original ways. Information is more than facts to recall for an exam and then forget. Facts offer data to analyze, view in new ways, and use to solve problems. As a result, these individuals work harder, longer, more thoroughly, and create more novel and effective solutions to problems than do their age-mates.

Gifted young people achieve a great deal if they want to. In many ways, however, they closely resemble their age-mates. They all have feelings, emotions, and preferences. They all feel excited, discouraged, calm or angry, confident or worried, depressed or bored. All show sensitivity to others and feel hurt by put-downs or coldness from those for whom they care. They all enjoy friends who genuinely like and appreciate them. Gifted youths share with all people the moods, sensibilities, and wishes for true friendship as well as for successful achievement.

These young people also enjoy many of the same activities as their friends. Playing athletic games, seeing interesting movies, listening to music, and sharing pizza with good pals satisfies them. All young people need fun and time out from work. Recreation means chances to do different things and use different parts of their personalities.

Like their peers, gifted youths look for their places in the world. All work to define themselves and to identify their beliefs, values, talents, and goals. All try to understand the ways in which they are unique and the ways in which they are similar to others. At the same time, all young people work at developing the necessary social, intellectual, and vocational skills that will allow them to accept responsibility for their own lives. In these ways, all adolescents have much to learn before reaching maturity.

Finally, all young people discover their strengths and limitations by testing themselves in the world. No one can do everything well, not even gifted people. Some topics come quickly. Others take more reading, thinking, and practicing before they can be mastered. Certain subjects always present difficulties to certain persons. Everyone excels at some things more than others, and this holds true for gifted youths, too. People can only do their best. Occasionally their best results in an exceptional outcome. More often, it does not. No one does everything perfectly, and no one does one thing perfectly all the time. Humans have limits. Maturity means recognizing, accepting, and working as effectively as possible within those limits. Again, gifted youths have much in common with their classmates.

Living with Giftedness   Giftedness becomes an important part of the way these young people see themselves. Understanding what this quality means sharply influences the way they know themselves and relate to their world.

They know that they differ from many classmates and wonder if this difference is all right. Is being different a good thing or a bad one? Gifted youngsters ask, ''Is it okay to be me?''

Elementary school-age children begin dealing with their differentness in their own ways. Scott, a very bright, creative, high-achieving fourth grader, realized that he and a friend were not as close as they had once been. Attempting to strengthen the friendship, Scott began listening to his friend's favorite radio station. He hoped this common interest would make the relationship more meaningful. After several weeks of tuning in, bored with what he heard and noticing no improvements in the relationship, Scott decided to turn the radio off. He was not happy going along with this friend's preferences simply to make the other boy like him better. Scott realized that he was a little different and became comfortable with his own style.

Teachers had been reading Nola's answers aloud to their classes for years. They used her English essays, history reports, and math problems as the standard of excellence to which all students should reach. While the praise and high achievement felt good to Nola, having teachers continually single her out separated Nola from her classmates. By junior high school she still performed at a superior level, but she was a lonely girl. Classmates thought she was too smart and too special to be interested in them. They did not often invite her to join in their fun. Behind her back, they mocked her as an ''egghead'' and turned her differentness into a barrier.

Nola's parents understood that ''peers'' did not necessarily mean those of the same age. Peers included persons who shared the same interests. Nola's parents encouraged her to participate in community groups with persons who could appreciate her talents rather than compete with them.

She joined her church's youth group, and her enthusiasm and resourcefulness soon moved her into leadership roles. Nola joined an adult folk-dance group, and her agility and energy allowed her to perform regularly at the group's shows. The friendship and encouragement she found outside school helped Nola feel at ease with herself and with her giftedness.

Liz focused her talents in social ways. She enjoyed people, and her fun-loving nature made her popular with her peers. She achieved well in school, dated the "right" people, and her originality enabled her to stand out from the crowd. For "Costume Day" in tenth grade, Liz appeared as Charlie Chaplin's "Little Chap" wearing a black derby, pencil mustache, and double-breasted suit, displaying a walking cane and a stiff-legged strut. By noon everyone in the school knew who she was and wanted to meet her. Liz's differentness brought her admiration rather than resentment because she entertained. She did not compete; she amused. All could enjoy Liz even as she was enjoying herself.

During the year Liz became involved in dramatics and spent more time with the Thespians, a theater club, than with her popular friends. She began to notice how the drama students sought uniqueness as a badge of honor. They prized eccentricity and used differentness to develop characters in their plays. In contrast, her old friends began to resemble carbon copies of each other. They wore similar clothes from the same stores. They went to the same parties with the same crowd. They did predictable things. Her popular friends laughed at anyone not belonging to their little group. Until now, Liz realized, she too had been like that.

The old friends could not understand what Liz found attractive about her new friends. One young man commented, "Why do you spend so much time with those people? You used to *BE* someone!"

Liz discovered that being herself was more interesting than being like everyone else. She deliberately began choosing friends whom she could like, respect, and appreciate for being themselves rather than because they were part of the "in crowd," agreed with her views, or made her look popular.

Scott, Nola, and Liz learned to accept their giftedness and to accept themselves. They decided that they were okay people although different from others in some ways. Being different did not mean they were better in all things or even better in certain areas all the time. It did not mean they were morally or spiritually superior to anyone. Being gifted meant that they could often achieve certain ends if they chose to. They behaved as themselves, and this pleased them.

In order to see their differentness and themselves as acceptable, all three young people received strong support from parents, teachers, and peers encouraging them to be true to their individual natures. Young people need someone special in their lives telling them that being different is acceptable as long as you are yourself.

Supportive parents tell their gifted children that they have special learning abilities. Everyone has strengths, weaknesses, and personal interests. Being yourself is important. If you happen to be a fast, curious learner, be one. If you solve problems creatively, do so. Sometimes you will not want to shine in class. Other times you will not be able to shine, because not even gifted persons can excel in everything or all the time. Wise parents tell their gifted children that they can only do their best and let the outcome take care of itself.

Encouraging parents only expect their gifted children to

be honest with themselves and to do their best. They stand behind their children and want to help whenever or however they can. At times these young persons know more about a particular subject than do the adults. Then parents encourage them to explore further with additional resources. These parents love the young persons for themselves, not for what they can do or for making the parents look good by their achievements. Whatever the results, these parents express love and appreciation to their children for doing their best.

Supportive teachers enjoy the interesting questions that gifted young people ask. They find that the questions make them think harder and bring the subject alive for the entire class. If the teachers do not know the answer, they do know where to find it or can suggest books for the interested young person to read about the subject. Encouraging teachers also ask questions of gifted youths to help them find the relationships among the facts, make generalizations, look for implications, and make the subject more meaningful. Teachers give assignments requiring analysis and putting information together in original ways. They expect gifted students to use ordinary knowledge to create new knowledge rather than asking for more of the same. These teachers show their students the benefits to all of attending class with gifted peers. They aim for increased understanding rather than competition.

In addition, supportive peers help gifted young people feel good about themselves and their differentness. Scheduled together in accelerated "Block," "Tag," or special classes, the young people encourage each other to be curious, creative, and achieving. The group shares intellectual talent and takes pleasure in using it. Aware that they all have excellent minds, they learn energetically without fear of alienating friends or feeling strange. High achieve-

ment becomes acceptable and expected in this group because everyone present can reach the goal. Programs such
as the Governor's School for the Gifted, science fairs, and
forensics and debate competitions offer other acceptable
channels for gifted young people to use their talents fully
and gain their peers' recognition and approval for doing
well.

With encouragement from parents, teachers, or classmates for being themselves, gifted youths learn that being
smart and creative is okay. Individual differences are acceptable. In fact, differentness offers satisfaction and ben-
efit to the individual as well as to others. When young
people accept themselves and believe in the value of being
who they are, peer pressure presents no problems. Like
other adolescents who know and live with their own personalities, attitudes, values, and talents, self-accepting
gifted adolescents have confidence in their abilities and decisions. They freely choose to spend time alone or with
friends. Their peers, likewise, understand and respect them
as individuals.

If peer influence impacts these gifted youths at all, the
effect is positive. The group still holds the center of much
activity for adolescents. The group encourages gifted youths
to socialize more, to leave the books and come out to the
Friday night basketball game or the Post-Exam Jam. The
good feelings from belonging and having fun lead once-
solitary gifted adolescents to become school yearbook pho-
tographers, join field hockey teams, or run for class offices. In these ways, they act independently and at the same
time as part of a team. They develop the social side of
their personalities and become happier people.

The Bright Group and Peer Pressure   Not all gifted adolescents feel comfortable with themselves. Like most

people their age, they look to understand the ways in which they differ from others and how they are alike. All work to develop the intellectual, social, and vocational skills needed to mature.

Having the label "gifted" confuses many young people. They misunderstand what giftedness means. Since much of who they are relates to the "gifted" tag, these adolescents have problems accepting themselves. For years parents and teachers have told them about their unlimited potential and how they could achieve great things. Gifted adolescents then ask, "Yes but *what* am I supposed to *do?*"

They wrongly believe that they can excel and accomplish much without first knowing themselves. They work seriously on their school assignments but never take time to get to know their own interests, attitudes, values, or feelings. They believe those qualities petty and unimportant. Ironically, those very personality factors provide the direction for the use of their intellect. Without self-awareness, gifted adolescents do not know on what to focus their talents. They stand with high expectations but no idea of where to go. Not accomplishing the great things expected, they silently wonder if they are losing their specialness. "Am I still gifted?" they ask. In this situation, they lose confidence in their own opinions and abilities and look to the group of other school-smart peers for support.

Gifted adolescents face another dilemma because they do not fully understand what giftedness means. They think they are supposed to learn everything quickly all the time. During elementary and junior high years, many learned everything fast. They heard the information once and knew the facts for the test. In high school and college, however, this changes. Courses now deal with more complex information and more of it. Gifted adolescents find they can no longer grasp all the data quickly every time they study. Work becomes more difficult, and the mastery grows slower.

Moreover, gifted adolescents discover that they can no longer be the best in everything because they have specialized talents and interests. They have a facility for science, for instance, but dislike the plodding pace they keep in literature. They do not realize that even gifted people must work hard on some topics before they comprehend the material. They can no longer be the best at everything or be the best at one thing all the time.

Once again, their expectations for success clash with what really happens. Once again, this situation shakes their confidence. They do not see themselves as slow learners, but now they learn more slowly. They do not see themselves as second-best in anything, but now they do not have the talent, time, or interest to be first in everything. As a result, they worry whether they are still special. To these confused young people, group membership becomes important.

Peer pressure acts as a potent factor in the lives of gifted adolescents unable to understand themselves fully and accurately. High-achieving, intelligent, ambitious students band together. They give one another support and approval. Their identity comes from their academic success, and they reinforce it by criticizing those who differ from themselves. The intelligent group laughs at socially popular peers, calling them superficial and ignorant. The bright students comment about the other group's emphasis on clothing, parties, and fake sophistication. They belittle the social group's slow wit and presence in "only average" classes. The bright group feels special again when they set up this unflattering comparison with their more outgoing but less academically talented classmates.

On the other hand, the bright group puts down the truly gifted among them. They see the most gifted classmates turning in exceptional work and receiving outstanding grades. Self-accepting, gifted adolescents at ease with themselves and their giftedness can take risks by asking far-out questions, challenging the teachers'. answers, or going alone to class activities. These young people do not seek or need their peers' approval before acting. They have a sense of who they are, where they are going, and what they are worth. Their self-assurance, purposeful actions, and high performance stand in sharp contrast with the bright group's high-potential-going-nowhere. In turn, the bright group acts competitively to shoot down their outstanding classmates. "Define that word. It's too hard for me," they complain sarcastically when Alice automatically uses her large vocabulary. "What's Alice trying to prove?" they whisper under their breath when Alice impresses them with her insightful and thorough work. The group implies that Alice deliberately tries to make them look bad by putting herself into the limelight. Others moan, "Sure she gets the best grade, but all she ever does is study," suggesting that Alice cannot be both high achieving and well rounded, with interests beside her books. In these ways, the bright group tries to justify their own lack of independence and unexceptional performance. Belittling their more confident and achieving peers makes them feel the group's support and makes their own intense striving or high achievement unnecessary.

In addition, the bright group wants to prove to themselves and to others that they are just as "normal" and fun-loving as any classmates. Labeled "different" for too long without understanding the commonalities among them and their contemporaries, they want to be "in," so they use their energies and talents to create supernormal entertainment. In recreation they can excel as they no longer do in the classroom. On weekends some use drugs or alcohol to get high, to challenge parental or societal authority, or to act in ways that they consider adult. They create wild parties by pushing their imaginations, opportunities, and luck too far. One group of the brightest students spending a chaperoned weekend away from home at a regional forensics competition smuggled beer into their hotel rooms and drank too much, and two boys landed in the hospital emergency room with broken arms after falling from second-story windows. Another group of honor roll fifteen-year-olds decided to conduct their own taste test of beer. They coaxed older friends to supply the beer and spent eight weekends in a row sipping it until giddy. They planned elaborate schemes for burying beer in the backyard and imaginative alibis explaining their behavior.

The bright group also explores sex as they try to prove their independence, specialness, and normality. Girls, especially, believe that they cannot be both brilliant and feminine. As a result, very bright young women often doubt their own attractiveness. They assume that their few-to-none dates reflect their lack of charm. Many need reassurance that they are lovely and desirable women. Bright young men, too, occasionally believe that succeeding in school is somehow unmanly. They need reassurance that they are just as masculine as their less achieving peers.

Explosive outcomes result as both bright young women and men seek approval for their sexual qualities as well as for their intellectual ones. Some act more intimately than the relationship calls for, wanting to become sexually involved to prove their sexual value. Others try out seductive behaviors in order to see what happens. They deliver come-on lines and flirt aggressively to prove they can act like "real" men or women. Sometimes they tease. Occasionally the adolescents find partners who will not allow them to back down on a sexual promise. For the brightest young people seeking more confidence in themselves, increased sexual activity provides a short-term way.

In groups, the brightest adolescents gain the same benefits from membership as do all young people. They feel appreciated, wanted, good about themselves, and learn how to behave in different situations. Nevertheless, the well-read high achievers know from their books or conversations with adults that peer groups often serve only as a crutch. To them, peer pressure looks like a cop-out preventing independent thought and action. Accordingly, these young people vigorously deny that the group influences them at all. They think of themselves as above peer pressure: they are too smart for that. Pointing to their social classmates, they say, "Now, there's peer pressure!" Their behavior, however, says something else. Because they feel uncertain about themselves and their gifts, group approval, support, and direction become very important to them.

The Bright Stars and Peer Pressure At times, gifted adolescents have mixed feelings about group membership. They want the bright or popular group's approval and acceptance but at the same time want to be special and separate. They seek to belong, but they also want recognition as "stars" for their high achievements.

Unlike those gifted adolescents who understand and feel at ease with themselves and act confidently without the group's blessing, these gifted individuals do not fully understand or accept themselves. They know the differentness but not the alikeness. They cannot be themselves because they believe that they are acceptable only as long as they achieve at a high level. Stars believe that when they do wonderful things, they, too, become wonderful. So much of who they are as individuals ties up with being gifted, and they mistakenly think they can be nothing else. They do not understand that even gifted persons cannot do all things excellently and cannot perform one thing excellently all the time. Nor do they understand how feelings, attitudes, and values play important roles in their lives.

In the past these stars received rewards mainly for high performing and received little for being themselves. They now feel driven to achieve. Their efforts and productions reflect great talent, but the way they show it reflects anxious, unsettled qualities. Stars appear to say, "Look at me!" one moment and nervously ask "I'm gifted, am I not?" the next. They never seem satisfied with their own accomplishments. After a monumental effort and a successful outcome, they cannot pat themselves on the back and rest awhile in the glow of achievement. Always stressed and agitated, they rush off to the next project. Stars feel only as worthwhile as their last major achievement.

Gifted stars never seem happy. They stand either under the pressure of putting together a magnificent project or under the pressure of finding another worthy task. Surprisingly, they tell you that their life lacks meaning despite all the achievements. Their lives seem to lack value because the stars look for significance in the wrong places. They seek meaning in the ends: the big show, the A term paper, the favorable election results. They do not look for importance in the process of putting a show together, gathering and relating information to tell an interesting story, or planning an effective campaign. After two months of grueling preparation, stars look for worthwhileness in the ninety seconds of applause and wonder why they feel cheated.

Even as the gifted stars receive little genuine satisfaction from their achievements, they take little pleasure from their relationships. Stars are lonely young people. They set themselves apart from groups in order to look special, but they bitterly resent their lack of acceptance by the groups of their choice. They very much want to be popular with the social group or respected by the gifted individualists. Yet they do not fit into either mold. They seek the spotlight but lack the confidence and self-awareness that would permit truly independent action. Friendly with many, they feel close to few. They make excuses for their lack of group acceptance, complaining that their maturity and talent are too complex for people their own age to appreciate.

As a consequence, all their achievements do little to build a solid sense of self-confidence. The stars feel dissatisfied with their accomplishments, dissatisfied with their relationships, and dissatisfied with themselves. Their expectations for themselves are unrealistic because they do not understand themselves. They feel only as worthwhile as their last prize, and they need to keep proving their worth. Their giftedness becomes the sole valuable characteristic they see in themselves. Unfortunately, they cannot find meaning in their actions, cannot continually shine in everything they do, and cannot count on dear friends for support and approval when they feel discouraged. To take off the mask of, "Hey, life's great and I'm great!" means losing face. They foolishly believe that truly gifted persons do not have doubts, feel discouraged, or need the comfort of caring people. The constant stress from unrealistic expectations for superior performance and the lack of closeness to caring peers or family mark gifted stars as candidates for suicide. The day they realize they cannot be Number 1 in everything, nothing else important exists in their life. Without the applause, they do not experience their own worth. When the pretense becomes too stressful, self-destruction sometimes appears as a possibility.

Gifted adolescents resemble other young people. All seek their places in the world and develop skills and attitudes by which to assume responsibility for their own lives. They all need to develop better understanding of their full personalities in order to identify how and where they wish to use their talents. Giftedness means that these young people differ in their learning capacities and thinking styles. In most ways they do not differ at all. Not understanding their uniqueness and their commonalities creates problems and leads many to rely on peer pressure for approval and direction.

Many people argue against placing gifted youngsters of the same high ability into school classes together. Instead, they propose sprinkling them through every classroom in mixed ability groupings. Putting gifted students together, they say, will make them into snobs. When they are with other young people as bright as they, they will all look down on the rest of us average folks who cannot keep up intellectually.

Positive peer pressure, however, works for gifted students when they are grouped together by ability in some classes. For some, this is the first time that their ideas have not been considered wild or weird. When they put two thoughts together in a new way, their classmates and teachers listen with appreciation and understanding rather than with the rolling eyes and shrugged shoulders of those who do not recognize creative thought when they hear it.

In classrooms for gifted students, it may be the first time some of these students have ever met a classmate smarter or cleverer than they. For once, they gain a more realistic notion of their own abilities and their own limits. They can appreciate and understand the frustration of not grasping a subject instantly and of having to work at comprehension. Coming up against some truly superior minds among their classmates, they can develop empathy and tolerance for those less sharp than they.

In addition, working in classes with other gifted students brings opportunities for all to discuss their feelings about being different. The loneliness, the left-out feeling when other students seem to have so many friends and so much fun, and the pressure from parents, teachers, and themselves to achieve at high levels are emotions and experiences that these youngsters can now share with each other. Through their sharing, they feel less alone and less confused about what giftedness means to them.

Far from building snobs, placing gifted students together exerts a positive peer pressure that makes them more self-understanding and self-accepting and better able to understand and accept others who are not like themselves.

Learning-disabled and Peer Pressure

Another 3 percent of the school age population[2] have difficulties with their differentness, too. Unlike the academically gifted young people, this differentness comes not from a wealth of talents but rather from a disturbance in the abilities they do have. These young people are learning-disabled.

Learning-disabled youths have been aware of their dif-

[2]Smith, David Gaddis, "Learning Disability a Success," *Daily Press*, November 6, 1981.

ferentness for a long time. Many found out their differentness when they began having trouble learning in school.
Many discovered their separateness when they could not
compete athletically with their classmates because they
were too clumsy or awkward. Others, unaware of any
difficulties, could not understand why classmates did not
want to be their friends. Likely to have average or above
average intelligence, they could not figure out how they
were different or what the differentness meant. They did
know, however, that in certain unpleasant ways they were
not like their peers.

These young people have difficulty understanding or
using language. They have problems with the mechanics
of receiving or processing information in their brains.
Thought requires the complex mixing of many small
steps: receiving clear information, relating it to other bits
of information, deciding how and how not to use it, and
applying it in action. Every small skill requires mastering
a series of many tiny steps in a certain order. Reading a
sentence or hammering a nail takes many small actions
using information that together makes up the whole.
Learning-disabled young people have a breakdown some-
where in the process. The problem may be small and
relatively minor. Some persons are unable to memorize
the complete multiplication tables. As long as they understand the numerical relations involved, a printed copy of
the times-tables helps them multiply successfully. Ways
exist to overcome certain limitations. On the other hand,
many learning-disabled persons have numerous small
breakdowns in the information processing path. The
more disabilities, the greater the handicaps, and the
greater frustrations that go along with them.

Learning-disabled young people are as different from
one another as they are from peers without these handi-

caps. Weaknesses appear in many ways. Stewart has difficulty hearing specific sounds and so has trouble speaking or reading correctly. Greg cannot distinguish the more important details from the less important ones and has trouble understanding what a story means, how to spell words correctly, or what his feelings tell him. Jack has a poor memory and cannot follow oral direction. Rob cannot think abstractly, so he cannot understand that actions now have consequences later. He cannot learn from experience to change his unsuccessful behaviors. With a short attention span, Rob cannot concentrate long enough to finish assignments or understand complex information. Other learning-disabled adolescents confuse left and right, ideas about time, or numbers.[3] Competent and able in many ways, these young people face overwhelming frustration in school unless they find alternative ways to grasp the material and complete assignments.

These disabilities also affect the young people's social behavior. Albert has poor ability to use his fingers and hands, so appears sloppy, with shirttail trailing outside his pants or shirt buttons pushed through the wrong holes. His hair looks uncombed or awkwardly arranged. Mason's speech sounds garbled or disjointed because of difficulty organizing his words. He uses the wrong words and has a small vocabulary. All this means that he cannot express himself clearly. Learning-disabled adolescents frequently cannot tell what they are feeling or ask for what they want.

Furthermore, their social behaviors turn off their peers. Learning-disabled adolescents act immaturely, inappropriately, and unpredictably.[4] Even though in his teens,

[3]Weiner, Judith, "A Theoretical Model of the Acquisition of Peer Relationships of Learning Disabled Children, *Journal of Learning Disabilities 13* (9) (November, 1980): 42–47.
[4]Ibid.

Tommy cries easily if disappointed or throws temper tantrums when frustrated enough. When Donna wants attention, she teases her classmates by pulling their hair or pinching the person whose attention she wants. Unlike their classmates, learning-disabled youths have not learned how to engage in conversation, wait for an opening, and then speak. When the other person responds to this behavior with surprise or disgust, they feel misunderstood and embarrassed. They cannot always understand the nonverbal message others send to them, so they regularly "misread" a situation and act in ways that appear strange. A teacher may sternly look at the individual and say, "Enough! One more word from you and that's it!" but the young person does not realize that this teacher means business. Naturally, the student interrupts the classroom again, and the furious teacher sends him or her out of the room.

With as much defeat as they experience academically and socially, and with so little opportunity to express their confusion, hurt, and anger, blowups occur. Exploding in rage, fists, or tears brings temporary relief. Learning-disabled youths act impulsively because they have no skills for time-consuming problem-solving.

On the other hand, withdrawing completely or running away from stressful events calms these individuals for a few moments. Unfortunately, these immature behaviors further disturb classmates. The learning-disabled adolescents appear to have lost all control of self and situation. They look weird and act crazy at the exact times when adolescents expect themselves to act cool and in charge. No wonder that few peers want to be their friends.

Learning-disabled young people face the same growing-up tasks that all adolescents face, but their differentness complicates the already difficult process. They

know they differ and that their differentness is not a good
one. Failure and blocks at school happen regularly. Many
do not behave like everyone else. They cannot act self-
assured. Whenever they build enough confidence to go
after what they want, they fall on their faces. Many see
themselves as failures, inept, ugly, and embarrassments to
their families. They believe they have nothing to offer
others. They hold low opinions of their own value. Many
learning-disabled youths cannot understand or accept
their handicap or work to make up for their limitations in
another way. Worst of all, everyone sees their failures.
Wanting the friendship and support that peer groups
provide, these young people despair of receiving that
acceptance.

Some learning-disabled adolescents readily find a
group that does accept them. Owen, for instance, has
minor handicaps: a poor memory for what he hears and
trouble moving his fingers in a coordinated way. Forget-
fulness or sloppy penmanship does not mark Owen as
terribly different from his classmates. He still performs
well in class, shows ability in sports, and learns the social
graces to make friends and maintain important relationships. He understands and likes himself. After all, he does
not seem so different from anyone else.

For adolescents with many learning disabilities, however, few choices for belonging remain. They can stay by
themselves, discouraged, and stop trying to win friends,
or they can join whatever group will have them. Many
unhappy, angry adolescents with low opinions of themselves find friends who make them feel better. They need
the social and emotional support in order to feel they have
value. Frequently they blame other people or the system
for their own failures. In a group, they can be angry
together. Too often, they direct their unhappiness to

destructive behavior. Needing to belong, they readily join the group in vandalism, drug use, or reckless behavior. Already impulsive, they are unwilling to risk the group's displeasure by saying, "No."

A recent federally financed study concludes that learning-disabled adolescents are more likely to become juvenile delinquents than teenagers without such disabilities. About 7 percent of learning-disabled teens become delinquents, compared with 4 percent for all teenagers.[5] Frustration from school and social failures and belief that they lack value and have no satisfying future ahead of them create reasons for these adolescents to act out hostility against their communities. Many feel they have nothing to lose; all seems already lost.

Being different complicates the process of growing up. When the differentness becomes a source of failure and humiliation, the task of understanding and accepting oneself grows more difficult. Without confidence in their ability to learn and be successful, learning-disabled youths fear change. They avoid learning the academic, social, and vocational skills needed to become mature adults. To them, learning most things means failure, and they are already sick of failing.

For years, professional educators did not fully understand or appreciate the problems learning disabilities created. Bright young people regularly failed to master certain tasks without recognizing the real issue. They did not realize that other learning channels could make up for the present limitations. Since 1970 professionals have discovered much to help learning-disabled youths to become successful learners and more socially confident persons. Learning-disabled young people need sensitive

[5]Smith, David Gaddis, "Learning Disabilities Haunt Some Delinquent Teenagers," *Daily Press*, November 5, 1981.

support in identifying, accepting, and adjusting to their disabilities. They require assistance, also, in seeing themselves as valuable, capable individuals in a future with few limits. In order to learn ways to compensate for their handicaps, they must first like themselves. Only confident individuals learn, and only confident individuals say "No!" to peer pressure.

For learning-disabled youths, positive peer pressure comes from learning to understand, accept, and overcome their special learning problems. Together in small resource classes one or two periods a day with specially trained teachers, these students can learn skills to overcome their weaknesses and can be successful. One small success encourages other learning-disabled classmates to build skills to make their own small successes. If one of them can do something good and right, there's a chance that each of them can learn skills to do something good and right, too. Those skills go with the young people into the regular classroom, making them feel less different and more acceptable to "regular" students.

Positive peer pressure works in other ways, also. When learning-disabled students have special talents in academics, sports, leadership, or such activities as photography, their learning problems are less visible. Their *abilities* become the focus of their peers' and teachers' attention. What they can do well, rather than what they cannot do well, is what others notice. Success in any one area of life encourages these young people to build skills to gain success in other areas. When friends and classmates see learning-disabled students as competent and able, these young people work up to the positive expectations.

Minorities and Peer Pressure

The United States is home for many minority groups.

Ethnic, religious, and racial groups the world over settled here and brought their uniqueness to the American "salad." Each minority member carries a special identity made of history, customs, and values prized by that group. Recognizing and living with these extra differences as well as with the individuals' own personality differences become tasks that adolescents face as they discover who they are.

Blacks represent one of the most visible minorities in the United States, making up about 12 percent of our population (1980 Census). For the sake of discussion, this survey of the effects of peer pressure on minorities looks at the ways adolescent Afro-Americans deal with this influence. Although the details of their experience are unlike those of other racial or ethnic groups, the process of becoming themselves in a complex adult world bears much in common with other minority group members' experiences.

Like gifted and learning-disabled young people, young Afro-Americans soon become aware of their differentness. Unlike the first two, however, the differentness is not based on learning ability or school performance. The differentness stems from a coincidence of birth. Skin color sets blacks apart from other Americans. An arbitrary characteristic unrelated to personal worth, ability, or achievement separates them. The historical facts of their presence in this country and the economic and psychological scars that many blacks develop as youngsters separate them, too. They know they differ but remain unsure what that differentness means.

All adolescents face the tasks of understanding their individual natures, accepting who they are, and building the skills that lead to an effective adulthood. Everyone differs, and everyone must learn to know and act on this uniqueness. When the larger society tinges the difference with racist slurs or suggestions that blacks are not good enough, young people question their own value. When the black society counters by saying, "Black is beautiful!" encouraging young people to take pride in their black heritage, young people question the white society's values. Knowing what to believe or be becomes more difficult for black adolescents, because too often they face an either-or choice: be black, or succeed and be white.

William Raspberry, a noted black writer, comments that too often our society narrowly defines "black." He notes that many black young people consider hard work and hard study to be "white" values. Trying to please the teacher is "white." Speaking correct English is "white." Waiting and preparing today in order to meet an important goal in the future is "white." Many attitudes and habits needed for success in school, business, and life are "white." Sadly, too many of us think that only outstanding talent in athletics, entertainment, and sex reflect valuable "black" qualities.[6]

Believing they must choose between remaining loyal blacks or betraying their own people puts many young Afro-Americans in a no-win position. At the very time when they should look for and develop their individual qualities, active voices in their minority culture tell them that they must remain true to their race and stay part of the group. If they hold true to their individual natures, they risk angering the group. Becoming friends with whomever they like, achieving highly in academic studies, displaying special talents appreciated by whites risk angering the group. As a consequence, peer pressure holds a strong influence among black adolescents.

Examples of Peer Pressure Among Black Adolescents   Young blacks have many ways of dealing with

[6]Raspberry, William, "'Black' Too Often Narrowly Defined," *Daily Press*, January 12, 1982.

peer pressure. The first way encourages the individual to give in to the group's influence and remain an active member. Aletha's approach illustrates this solution. She felt uncertain about the real meaning of her minority status. Deep down, she wondered if she was, indeed, not as good as whites, although she loudly told all listeners that she was better than her white classmates. She suspected that she had less intellectual ability than her white classmates because they did not seem to work hard to earn acceptable grades. Aletha believed that she had fewer chances to get ahead, fewer roads to advancement in the larger society.

These beliefs discouraged her. She did not put time and energy into improving her abilities. Aletha viewed luck and low effort as causing her lackluster achievements. She blamed the system for keeping her from accomplishing her goals, arguing that the deck of life's opportunities was permanently stacked against her. She refused to do her best on standardized tests given in school to measure academic progress, because she thought that since blacks always performed poorly on formal tests,[7] effort on her part would do little good. Everyone knew, she rationalized, that white people designed the tests, and the tests discriminated against blacks.

Aletha's low opinion of herself, her lack of the confidence needed to work up to her capacity, and her daily expectation of failure allowed her to "get by" with C and D work. The school placed her in less demanding classes equal to what administrators saw as her "tested" ability and observed achievement. Her parents and teachers did not want to push her above her intellectual level, so they did not enthusiastically demand more of her.

[7]Sattler, Jerome M., *Assessment of Children's Intelligence*, revised reprint (Philadelphia: W. B. Saunders Company, 1974). In addition to the strong white middle-class bias of standard tests noted by investigators, factors of low motivation to perform well on the tests, little test practice, poor reading skills, and lack of rapport with examiners enter into the low test scores of minority children.

The mediocre school achievement and the lack of any other outstanding characteristic made Aletha need her friends' support and approval even more. She did not feel competent to form her own opinions or challenge herself with new tasks. Privately she admitted that the schoolwork was too easy and that she knew she had more ability than she used, but she held it back. Often in class she knew an answer before her classmates, yet she remained silent. She did not allow herself to set high goals or strive to achieve anything beyond the minimum, because she feared that she would not be successful.

Even if Aletha could achieve more academic success, she did not want to jeopardize her friendships. When she studied seriously, her black peers looked suspiciously at her, asking, "Who do you think you are?" Once, when Aletha earned a higher grade, her friend picked the B+ paper off her desk, held it upside down by a corner as if it were a dead fish, and commented, "You think you're too good for us now?" Afraid the higher mark was beginner's luck, Aletha again chose group membership over working up to her abilities.

Aletha's group also influenced the choice of acceptable adults as mentors. One of her friends, Sheila, had many difficulties at home. Her family problems drained so much of her energy that her grades in junior high dropped sharply. Her teachers referred Sheila to the school psychologist for an evaluation so they might work with her more effectively. The psychologist, a white woman, took a personal interest in the troubled black girl and kept the supportive relationship going through the next six years.

In high school Sheila developed a relationship with another white adult, this time a teacher who talked with her often, cheering on her efforts to use her abilities well. Sheila deeply enjoyed these two relationships with caring adults but knew that her black friends disapproved. She valued the white adults who took a personal interest in her, but she felt guilty about feeling so loving toward anyone white. She thought no white people were supposed to be so important. Sheila felt torn between her group's values and her cherished relationships. As an answer to her dilemma, Sheila began making ugly comments about white people to her black friends. She tried to prove to her peers that she did not need white people even though she genuinely cared for two whites. Sheila prayed that her nasty remarks would not reach her white friends' ears.

Van's situation reflected another way of responding to peer pressure. He was a good-natured young black man. He had a fine singing voice and enjoyed music classes. Short and stocky, he became an able wrestler in his weight class with the help of his coach. He earned steady C's in his academic coursework.

Nevertheless, the black youths in his neighborhood did not want to spend time with Van. Van stuttered occasionally. When he sang, the defect disappeared into the melody and rhythm, but he spoke haltingly. Not handsome or cute, with his quiet personality he did not attract friends looking for a good time. Van wanted the company of black fellows, but he always remained on the sidelines. He was labeled weird, and others felt that association with him might make them look strange.

Several white groups at school viewed Van differently. The music students liked his voice and respected his ability to sing without piano accompaniment. The drama students respected his willingness to get on stage and be a character in *Oklahoma* and *West Side Story*. Van did not fear acting the clown or villain when given a script to read. He relished the attention when given permission through a play to ham it up. In addition, the athletes admired

Van's readiness to throw his all into a meet and his ability to master the finer techniques of his sport.

As a result, Van became an unofficial member of several white cliques. He spent time with them in class and in extracurricular activities. To the white kids, Van was interesting, and they welcomed him to their lunch tables and their school activities. Van did not develop deep personal relationships with his white friends, but he did share their company at school. He felt pleased about himself, flattered that some people finally noticed and appreciated his qualities.

In a different approach to dealing with peer pressure, Rodney showed a way to break away from the group's control without angering his black friends. A young man of considerable talent, Rodney saw his blackness as part of himself, a characteristic of which to be confident and proud. He was confident and proud of his other qualities. He took advanced classes in all subjects and earned excelent grades. An understanding listener, he became a resourceful and popular leader respected by both blacks and whites. Rodney believed in his abilities, his purposeful efforts to achieve his goals, and his own value as an individual.

Blacks as well as whites enjoyed Rodney's company, and the young man treated all with ease and appreciation. He lived in a mainly black neighborhood but attended classes with many whites. At dances, he chose partners of both races. He went to black friends' parties and white friends' parties. He felt comfortable in any group. The whites liked his personality and respected his intelligence and leadership skills. The blacks enjoyed his company and respected the fact that Rodney took pride in his blackness and made time for his black friends.

Rodney had a lot of help achieving peace with himself.

His family always encouraged him to be himself and to follow his own gifts. If he had an effective manner with people, he should develop the talent as far as he could. If he had scholastic ability, he should develop that as far as he could. His family stressed the need for him to be true to himself and to accept all that he was. Blackness was his proud heritage, but his future rested on his own talents and hard work. With his family's continued interest and encouragement, Rodney found their faith in him strengthened his determination to excel. His family's opinion of him became more valuable to him than his friends' views. The family's confidence gave him the strength to be a friend but not to be ruled by his friends' opinions.

Rodney took care, though, that his black friends knew how much he prized them. He made time to spend with them, and he never took his acceptance by whites too seriously. Always conscious of his race, Rodney balanced the different aspects of his personality without denying expression to any. Blackness was part of who he was, and he wanted black friends with whom to share this important aspect of his experience in the world. There were parts of his life that only they could fully understand.

In addition, Rodney regularly succeeded in school and was popular with people. He expected to do well and had the confidence to use his abilities effectively. He realized quickly that ability and effort could earn him what he wanted. He had realistic ambitions for college and a professional degree, and he willingly put the effort into achieving his long-range goals.

Accepting all facets of himself and self-assured, Rodney became an outstanding person because of his differences. Like any mature person, he could be part of a group but not hostage to it. He knew what his friends expected, and in turn they knew what he expected: the freedom to be himself as well as one of them.

In another approach, Nadine chose the most difficult courses in school and performed highly in them all. Popular with her white classmates, she won election to class office and served in many community organizations. She wanted to become a physician, and she had the energy, intelligence, and personality to make that goal a reality. All her actions seemed to reflect success and self-confidence.

Nevertheless, she did not truly feel at ease with herself. All her friends were white, and she kept a cool distance from everyone. She attended parties and school dances but danced only with white boys. In tenth grade when a popular black classmate invited her to the movies, she turned him down. Another well-liked black youth asked her to go to the basketball tournament with him one Christmas, and she said, "No, thanks." Soon the word among the black students was that Nadine thought she was better than they were. They sneered that she wished she were white, and they left her alone.

Nadine felt greatly relieved when the black students stopped bothering her. She did not feel like one of "them" anyway. Yet while white boys danced with her at school, and white groups included her in many of their activities, they never asked her for a solo date. Nadine had no close girlfriends of either color. She said her busy schedule did not leave time for chit-chat. With many people around, Nadine remained very much a loner.

Nadine viewed her racial identity as simply an accident of birth. Her blackness had nothing to do with her. She said heredity made her black; it was nothing over which she had any control. She would not allow the despair of generations to keep her down. Nadine wanted to escape from her skin color through strong achievement and gaining whites' friendship. She almost felt as if she were white because she excelled at "white" activities and had "white" values. She did not feel like a black person, implying that blacks as a group were not as able, worthy, or successful as she would like to be. Nadine never truly accepted her racial identity as a valuable aspect of herself.

Nadine had difficulty accepting herself as she was—a talented, young black woman. She feared that the racial stereotypes might be true, and she did not want to find in herself those negative characteristics attributed to blacks by several hundred years of white racists. She falsely assumed that her blackness was a handicap, and she refused to accept it as a positve part of herself. Thus, she never really relaxed. She always felt on guard, ready to prove her talents as a way to reassure herself that she was competent and accomplished.

Aletha, Sheila, Van, Rodney, and Nadine, like all adolescents, were learning about themselves and building the skills to be responsible adults. They each had individual differences, which they needed to recognize and develop fully. Physical racial characteristics were part of these differences, and each young person decided what it meant to be a black person in this society.

Only Rodney and Van accepted their black identity without defensively needing to prove anything. They knew themselves to be no better or worse than whites. They were just themselves and respected all their friends as individuals. They liked whom they liked, regardless of skin color. They strove for excellence and associated with whites without feeling as if they constantly betrayed their racial group. At the same time, Rodney genuinely enjoyed his black friends' company without making apologies to anyone. He had the skills and confidence to be himself. Aletha and Sheila lacked confidence to be themselves and allowed the group to make many of their decisions about achievement and friendships. Nadine did not have the confidence to accept all her attributes, only those that she thought would bring approval in the white world. None of the three could honestly accept themselves or their racial identity without excuses, bravado, or denial.

For minorities, positive peer pressure comes in a variety of ways. Many Asian students, for example, come from homes that value hard work and high achievement in education as a way to be successful in adult life. These children study long hours and encourage others from Asian families to work hard and to be the best students they can be. They often study together to feel less lonely and cut off from social life, and they help each other with difficult coursework. If these teens earn the highest test scores, bring in the most complex and outstanding projects, and receive acceptance to the prestigious colleges and universities, it is not because they are the smartest students. It is because they work the hardest at their studies.

For blacks, positive peer pressure comes from other black students who also value setting goals for the future, working hard, and achieving highly. It can also come from friends of any race and culture who share the same values of setting and achieving meaningful personal goals through hard work and high achievement.

Positive peer pressure comes from having friends who share your constructive values. Teens want to make themselves happy, and they want to please their friends, too. When teens choose friends who want to accomplish good things and make good things happen for themselves and for others, they influence each other to those ends.

Conclusion

Everyone differs. Everyone has unique skills, personalities, and family histories. Finding, understanding, and living successfully with these differences is what adolescence is all about.

Gifted, learning-disabled, and minority young people face their differentness sooner than do most adolescents. Their unusual characteristics make them stand out and receive special attention from the earliest years. Others respond to these differences with a wide range of reactions. Onlookers express puzzlement, pleasure, pride, shame, or anger at these differences. Does the differentness make them better or worse than anybody else? Does it provide more chances to be happy or cruelly shut more doors in their faces?

Learning to identify, understand, and work effectively with—or in spite of—these characteristics challenges young people. When the important adults in their lives encourage them to know, like, and fully express themselves, special qualities included, the chances for building self-confidence and effective skills increase. When the influential people in their world ignore, belittle, ridicule, or resent those traits, the likelihood of the young people's doing the same increases. Without the capacity to know and like themselves, these special young people cannot build the assurance or skills necessary to become independent adults. Without self-confidence and well-developed skills, these adolescents depend heavily on their peer groups for support, acceptance, and advice. The group that lets them be members becomes all-important and provides the rules for making decisions about clothing, recreation, friendships, achievements, and lifetime goals.

Peer pressure costs a lot for these young people. For the

gifted, not understanding the meaning of their talents wastes a precious human resource. Uncertain of themselves, they need the group's approval too much to risk individuality. If they do achieve highly, they do so at tremendous emotional cost and risk unhappy or shortened lives.

Learning-disabled adolescents, embarrassed about their poor performance in school or social shortcomings, frequently do not let themselves discover alternative ways of learning. Not understanding their handicaps, they cannot use their average or above average intelligence in constructive ways. Feeling incompetent and worthless, they seek acceptance whenever they can find it. They usually find it among other angry, blaming persons. The cost of delinquency and adult crime to the larger society is at least as great as the untallied costs of wasted, unhappy lives.

Minority group young people who do not see their ethnic, religious, or racial characteristics as acceptable differences offering a special richness to their lives also depend heavily on peer approval. Unless they accept and become all of themselves, differences included, they lack the confidence needed to develop effective intellectual, decision-making, or interpersonal skills.

More than most adolescents, those with special differences require additional encouragement from persons in their lives. For a long time, their qualities marked them as separate. Now these youths need to address directly what these qualities do mean and get rid of misinformation about what they do not mean. Fears, thoughts, and expectations about their differentness should be openly discussed. Adolescents must know and understand themselves before they can build the confidence and expertise to move beyond the group and into their true individuality.

Independence and Responsibility

Young people accomplish a great deal before becoming adults. They learn about their own beliefs, values, feelings, interests, and abilities. They find their strengths and their limitations. They learn ways to get along with the different people in their lives. They learn how to behave as independent persons in various situations. They pick vocational directions and start building skills necessary to reach their goals. They face major losses and disappointments, make major choices and lesser ones. Throughout adolescence, young people discover how to make sense of a complex, changing world and how to conduct themselves in it.

Today's adolescents face many difficult tasks. Society sets high expectations for young people and sets equally high stakes. The time to develop a philosophy of life and adopt the problem-solving skills that affect a lifetime begins. Behaviors have outcomes. Choices have consequences. No wonder so many young people feel unready for the challenge. In fact, one young person in ten has a problem meeting the demands of growing up that requires professional help.[1]

Independence and responsibility mean making effective

---

[1] Weiner, Jerry M., "Introduction: Adolescent Psychiatry Today," in Joseph R. Noveiil, ed., *The Short Course in Adolescent Psychiatry* (New York: Bruner/Mazel, 1979).

decisions, acting on one's own judgment, and living gracefully with the consequences. Generally, the more effective the choice, the more satisfying the result. Poor choices lead to unhappy consequences and, it is hoped, to better decisions in the future. Growing up signifies learning how to make sound decisions and bring about desired ends. This process takes time, thought, and experience. Adulthood does not arrive automatically with the eighteenth birthday.

Many young people cry for their independence without giving a thought to their responsibility. They want drivers' licenses, spending money, jobs, the right to pick their own friends, and privacy. They do not consider their end of the bargain. For instance, they want the right to drive the family car but fail to pay for the gas they burn, to schedule the car's use so as not to inconvenience other family members, or to drive safely within the limits of legal or personal competence. Too many young people act impulsively without waiting to define better solutions. Maturity means considering one's own interests, present and long-term, as well as others' interests before acting.

Belonging to a group helps adolescents to meet their needs for independence. With friends who encourage and agree with them, young people go into the world without their parents. The group decides how to think, what to value, which activities, goals, and friendships matter, and the unique style in which to carry out their plans. The group determines the why's and how's that help its members build confidence in themselves when away from home. Belonging to a group offers steps on the way to maturity.

Although groups offer a form of independence from parents, they do not offer true independence. Independence signals that the decisions and the behaviors belong to the individual. It means no one controls these people, neither parents nor group. Independent persons truly direct themselves and rely on their own judgment.

No one, however, stands totally independent. We live in a world with other people we need. We love them or require their goods or services. We must consider those people in our decisions if we desire continued, mutually satisfying relationships. Likewise, we would like others to consider us when they make decisions about their lives. If people thought only about themselves and their own immediate gain when making decisions, they would turn the world into a selfish, lonely, chaotic place. Caring, concern, and courtesy would disappear. Societies and civilizations would fall as people no longer worked for common goals. Although outsiders do not rule our choices or make our decisions for us, they remain vital factors to consider when we make choices. The choices remain ours, the responsibility remains ours, but we are not the only persons involved in our decisions.

People account for their actions. They answer to themselves when the results of a poor decision turn out harmful, unpleasant, or ineffective. Choices made in haste or for short-run gain often become long-run problems. We cannot rightfully blame unpleasant consequences on other people, wrong timing, unfortunate circumstances, or plain bad luck. Like a boomerang, poor decisions swing back to us. Whether we like it or not, legally, morally, and personally, we answer for our choices.

Groups, on the other hand, are not accountable. When everyone is to blame, no one is to blame. Following the group's wishes, young people do not risk making their own decisions. In their minds, they need not accept responsibility for their actions. Although group membership offers a positive alternative to young adolescents wanting to build skills and confidence apart from their families, allowing the group to decide keeps adolescents from earning their maturity.

Adulthood requires independence and responsibility. Adulthood requires making effective decisions and living with the outcome. Mature young people remain group members, but they also assert themselves as separate individuals. For mature adolescents, the group provides entertainment and friendship. Now, however, the individuals themselves choose when to go along and when to stand apart. Mature adolescents can stay or leave because they have moved beyond peer pressure.

Ways to Move Beyond Peer Pressure

Although group membership holds importance during early adolescence, strict obedience to group values and actions lessens as young people gain increasing skills and confidence with which to take charge of their own lives. The changes do not happen quickly or in obvious ways. Over time, the adolescents move from dependence on the group for identity and direction to mature independence and responsibility. Many strategies build the skills and confidence necessary for this growth.

Knowing Themselves   Not all adolescents understand their own personalities. Until this time, they have not had the abstract mental powers to stand back and observe themselves. Their parents have always told them what to think or how to behave. Next, the group provided similar direction. Few young people have taken the opportunity to wonder what they really feel or believe about a situation. Without enough real-world experience to rely on their own perceptions or judgments about the way things appear, they do not trust themselves. They do not place enough confidence in their own feelings or thoughts to allow acting on them.

Young people need to know and understand their own feelings, beliefs, values, and preferences. When an event occurs, they need to ask, "What do I think about this?" "How does this square with my beliefs about the world and my place in it?"

"In what ways does this incident suggest that I should revise my thinking, or suggest that I was right?"

"What do my feelings tell me? What aspect of this situation makes me feel uneasy, angry, elated, or doubtful?"

"How do my present feelings fit with my beliefs? If they do not agree, what should I do?"

Every event provides an occasion to reflect and see where they stand. Knowing themselves clarifies decisions and plans and makes the outcome more beneficial.

Knowing themselves also requires recognizing their abilities and limits. Certain tasks come easily, whereas others take repeated practice. Knowing which are which allows better planning for their use. If mastering math presents greater difficulties than reading essays, allowing more time for arithmetic homework than English assignments makes sense. Likewise, knowing their particular physical limits permits effective planning. Recognizing when they feel too tired to study efficiently or when they are too groggy to drive a car safely represents internal controls by which adolescents monitor themselves. Knowing their emotional limits means accepting the discomfort in the pit of the stomach, the tight throat, or the nervously tapping foot as signs before words that something upsets them. Instead of ignoring the signs, wise young people ask, "What does this feeling tell me?" Then they look to the actual cause for answers.

Knowing themselves takes quiet time, experience, and

much reflection. Busy, hectic schedules do not permit this activity. Reflective thinking occasionally leads to uncomfortable awarenesses that some would rather avoid. For instance, one view of events may no longer be accurate although once it was fine. New insights may clash sharply with ideas presently held. At times new awarenesses about who they are means changing old beliefs and adopting different, more effective, and genuine ways of being themselves. This means weighing the evidence and making decisions. It leads to growth, maturity, and responsible choices.

Knowing themselves fully and honestly becomes a lifelong process. Frequently the task proves difficult. The rewards, however, include deeper satisfactions from wiser decisions. Without knowing themselves, adolescents do not recognize what they believe, understand what they value, or know what they want. For these unaware young people, going along with the group on every issue provides the only clear direction.

Forming and Testing Their Own Opinions Everyone has opinions. Some consider studying to be a meaningful experience, whereas others think of school strictly as a place to visit friends. Some believe in early curfews on weekdays; others don't. Politics, religion, social customs, art: pick a topic and find many different viewpoints about the "right way" to consider it.

Adolescents, too, have opinions. Most start by repeating their parents' beliefs about events. When they become group members, they voice the group's views about "the proper way." As they mature, young people begin forming more of their own beliefs about the world. Experiences they now have force them to look at their values and make decisions about where they stand. Young people observe friends making choices and ask themselves if they would handle the matter in the same way. Capable of increasingly abstract thinking, adolescents mull over the "What if's," speculating about the possibilities for action if certain events happened to them.

As they mature, young people form more individual ideas about the world and beliefs about correct thought and action. They remain unsure, however, about the validity of their opinions. They wonder if their beliefs make sense. They wonder if their ideas sound credible and workable. For awhile, adolescents keep their personal opinions to themselves. They go along with the group, doubting the wisdom of their own judgment.

Confidence takes time to grow. Young people lack the confidence to voice or act on their own opinions. Some young people believe that the worth of their views depends on the force of their arguments rather than on the sound-ness of their reasoning. They speak loudly and rapidly, conveying strong determination. Unfortunately, they do not listen thoughtfully to opposite viewpoints or consider con-trary evidence. These adolescents suspect that finding merit in alternate perspectives represents weakness, and they do not want to appear uncertain or indecisive.

Nevertheless, expressing their opinions aloud builds confidence in their effective reasoning skills. Actively dis-cussing issues with parents, teachers, or friends helps young people test their thinking skills and weigh their conclu-sions. Vigorous debate provides a chance to spell out their thoughts and look at all sides of the issue. Speaking hon-estly with objective outsiders allows adolescents to feel free to consider all the evidence and revise their opinions with-out losing face. When a respected person takes their opin-ions seriously and give merit to their reasoning, young people begin respecting their own opinions, too. When they respect their own judgment, they gain the self-assurance to put their views into action.

Adults assist adolescents to learn effective reasoning skills by giving them credit for their convictions and recognizing the soundness of their arguments. Complex issues include many positive and negative facets. Mixed views about difficult topics result. Adults help adolescents by recognizing the value in their beliefs even when disagreeing with their conclusions. Wise adults prevent the issue from becoming a win-or-lose contest. They realize that two persons often view the same scene from varying vantage points. Total agreement is not a goal. Understanding the other's opinions is. Different opinions stated calmly and reviewed without pressure to agree leaves room for the two parties to consider all the ideas without appearing weak. They can assess the evidence without feeling indecisive, and they can form the most appropriate opinion for themselves.

Developing Skills   Adolescents have a lot to learn. They must learn many intellectual, social, and vocational skills. They must learn to understand themselves as individuals. They must learn the decision-making process. Young people must find their natural abilities and talents and work toward developing greater expertise in them.

People judge successful ends as the results of four interacting factors: ability, effort, task difficulty, and luck. When adolescents work to refine and enhance their abilities, they depend more on their skills and their own efforts. They rely less on picking the easy path or trusting to luck to accomplish their goals. Greater skills spell increasing mastery of their own lives and increased self-confidence to handle whatever life brings.

Many opportunities exist for developing abilities. The

group brings occasions to build social skills in conversation, understanding different viewpoints, and gaining empathy for others. School provides chances to build intellectual, problem-solving, and communication skills as well as to learn attitudes and techniques needed for satisfying careers. Recreation brings times for enhancing athletic, artistic, and interpersonal skills. Every new situation equals another opportunity to practice sizing up an event and determining the most appropriate action.

Practice brings better skills. Better skills bring young people additional confidence and effectiveness in their dealings with people and events. We are what we do. When we act capably, we show greater effectiveness as persons.

Learning How to Make Decisions and Making Them Knowing and understanding themselves becomes especially important to young people at decision-making time. Unlike pin-the-tail-on-the-donkey, making decisions should not resemble a blind, confused stab at a desired goal. Effective decision-making is not impulsive. It consists of a five-step process that requires patience, abstract thinking, and a deep awareness of one's own values and priorities.

Identifying the main issue comes first. What is the problem? When does it happen? Who else is involved? Answering these questions requires stepping back and calmly viewing the situation. For instance, Susan considered breaking up with Frank because, in her opinion, he did not treat her fairly. He expected her always to be ready for him, yet he frequently spent time with his buddies away from her. When Susan made plans with her girlfriends, on the other hand, Frank was furious. Susan's resentment increased, and she was ready to call the relationship quits.

Next, young people must look at possible alternatives

and their consequences. Then they determine how each outcome fits with their own values and priorities. If Susan told Frank to take a long walk, she might not find another boyfriend for awhile. Frank might feel disappointed at the loss of this valued relationship with her. The decision might anger some of Frank's friends who thought Susan treated Frank unfairly. If Susan decided to continue the relationship as it existed, she might become still angrier and more resentful until she poisoned the relationship with bitter sarcasm or rudeness. She might dislike herself for not voicing her beliefs. Since Susan prized her honesty and self-respect, she realized that she could not remain with Frank as things now stood.

Third, young people must decide what comprises the next step. Susan decided to tell Frank kindly but firmly about her feelings and suggest ways to improve their relationship. In this way she could keep her self-respect and be honest with herself and Frank. She could also attempt to keep the relationship but in a more satisfying arrangement.

Fourth, the time comes to act upon their choices. Susan told Frank she would like to discuss an important matter with him. She arranged to meet in a quiet, private place where they could talk without interruption.

Fifth, individuals must weigh the results. Frank told Susan that he valued his friends and her, too. He did not think he acted selfishly. He expected her to wait until he wanted to see her. Susan told him that although she enjoyed his company, she no longer wanted to continue the relationship like this. Although Susan felt nervous telling Frank her feelings, she experienced tremendous relief once she had spoken. They agreed to see less of each other and to begin dating other people.

In the following days Susan felt more certain that she

had made a wise choice. Her resentment and anger left, she spent time with her girlfriends, and she began relationships with several interested young men. Susan also grew more confident about her ability to act on her beliefs and to resolve difficult situations.

The process of making decisions remains the same regardless of the details involved. Whether the central problem involves a relationship or a career choice, the steps follow in logical order. Thinking about all the issues, alternatives, and consequences sometimes seems confusing. Seeing how outcomes fare in view of personal values is difficult. At times, finding a trusted listener helps to sort out the issues and feelings and clarifies the whole situation.

No guarantees exist for perfect solutions every time, but carefully thought-out decisions bring less regret later than do hasty ones. Doubts remain. Second-guessing is natural. If the solution turns out less satisfying than expected, the person can review the factors once more and revise the plan. Even no decision becomes a decision to continue things as they are. People can only make the best decisions they can.

When young people make thoughtful decisions, they act to influence their own lives. In this way, they behave independently and responsibly. They build confidence in their own ability to take command of their lives. Assured in their ability to make good decisions, adolescents become less dependent on peer pressure.

Not Fearing Mistakes   No one gets everything right the first time. People cannot improve unless they risk making mistakes and learning from their errors. Persons judge a situation, select what they believe to be the most appropriate action, put the plan into effect, and see what results.

They then decide how effective their solution appears. If the results satisfy, they chose well. If the results fall short of the desired outcome, people review their decision. They determine what factors might have been considered further and what might have been tried differently. After this first attempt at a solution, they have a better idea of the whole situation and a more informed notion of what plan will work. They keep what works and revise parts that do not. Then they test the new plan. People are not perfect, and neither are their answers to life's problems. If the first thoughtful answer does not work, at least they have come closer to a solution that will.

Many adolescents fear making mistakes. They think mistakes lead to disappointments, setbacks, ridicule, disapproval, and wasted time. They think that mistakes mark them as failures, and no one likes to feel worthless. Believing this, young people avoid testing their ideas or actions in the world. They miss receiving the feedback from their actions that would enable them to be more effective the next time. They do not learn, and they do not improve their understanding or their skills. Finally, those afraid to make mistakes cannot build the self-confidence to act as independent adults.

Of course, not all things need testing. Driving a car at ninety miles an hour at night on a rain-slicked road may lead to serious injury or death. Mixing drugs and alcohol at a party may spell a fatal coma. Some mistakes are deadly. Physical danger is one thing; disappointment or a neighbor's eyebrows raised in disapproval are another. Young people know the difference, and they can permit mistakes in situations when lack of success does not become life-threatening.

When adolescents do not fear making mistakes, they see themselves as competent individuals not desperately in need of another's protection in order to feel safe. They have confidence in themselves and do not need the group's good opinion. Confident young people have the desire to learn new skills and try new tasks because they expect successful outcomes. If the results do not seem perfect the first time, they will improve the next.

Confident adolescents keep their sights high and expect more of life than settling for the sure thing. They select the challenging yet possible way in career choices and in relationships. They accept responsibility for their actions and do not blame the environment or other people for their own shortcomings. These adolescents look realistically at themselves and use their abilities effectively. They view mistakes as steps to greater mastery and use their experiences to improve their skills.

Keeping Their Friends But Following Their Own Lead   Friends are important to us. They entertain us when we feel bored. They understand us when no one else seems to. They offer suggestions when we wonder what to do next, and they offer comfort when we feel discouraged. They have answers for our doubts and applause for our triumphs.

Good friends also allow us to disagree with them occasionally and to have our own thoughts. No two people agree completely on all topics all the time. People build strong relationships on bonds of trust and respect. These ties can stand the tugs and pulls of persons who view the world differently yet who wish to understand the other's ideas. Friends work toward goals they both want while allowing for individual uniqueness. In fact, these differences make the friendship more exciting as each tries to grasp the other's viewpoints. In the process, they sharpen and expand their own.

For adolescents, the group holds much meaning, but young people need to find ways to belong as well as to behave independently. Increasingly, they have and express their own views on issues arising in the group. More and more, they act on their own initiative without first consulting their friends. Keeping their friends' approval begins to matter less than acting responsibly on their own judgment.

As they mature, young people continue to join group activities for the fun, fellowship, and caring relationships. At different times, they choose to be alone or with persons outside the group. Older adolescents seek the social space permitting both membership and the freedom to leave. Relationships with friends change from early to late adolescence. Individual decisions increasingly replace group wisdom as the basis for action. Needing less approval from their friends, they become more interesting and separate individuals. They appreciate and enjoy each other's differences rather than seek safety in their similarities.

Linking Independence and Responsibility   As adolescents mature, they make more effective decisions in all areas of their lives. Understanding that they must live with the consequences of their actions, they learn to select alternatives responsibly. If a plan falls short of the desired end, they revise their strategy next time. Meanwhile, young people know they must make the best of the situations in which they place themselves.

This approach represents a marked change from the way young adolescents view independence. To children, independence means acting without parents' constant supervision. It means taking on the symbols of adulthood—cigarettes, cars, dating, alcohol, sex—without building foundations of sound judgment regarding time, place, purpose, or amount. Like ripe apples bursting with sweetness on the backyard tree, children see independence as prizes to be picked and eaten. They do not notice the complex root system or the sturdy trunk and limbs supporting the full branches. Without the mature tree, no apples grow. Likewise, without a basis in the skills, knowledge, effective decision-making, and self-confidence needed to act as responsible individuals, no independence becomes possible.

To gain real maturity, adolescents link independence and responsibility. If they want telephone privileges to speak with friends privately in the evening, for example, they use the phone responsibly. They keep the call short to permit other family members to make and receive calls. They tell their friends not to call after a specified hour so as not to awaken sleeping relatives. If young people want the right to drive the family car for school or social activities, they pay for the gas they use, plan ahead to see if their intentions for the car fit with other family members' plans, return home when expected, and drive safely. Adult behavior and adult responsibility go together if young people learn the true meaning of maturity.

Parents help adolescents connect independence and responsibility. Adults help when they set reasonable rules to guide young people's behavior. They decrease the limitations as their children show success in accepting increased responsibilities along with their freedoms. Supportive adults view limits as ways to reinforce adolescents' obligations to themselves and others. Rules do not mean control agents or symbols of power. Especially when parents and adolescents together determine and agree to the rules, young people expect to follow them.

In addition, wise parents give their growing children encouragement and opportunities to act maturely on their own and live with the outcome. The exact opportunities depend on the young person's age and maturity. When an adolescent fails a school course because of repeated absences, for instance, supportive parents allow the young person to fail. They do not race to the principal with false excuses for the absences. Helpful parents do not rescue their children from the natural consequences of their acts. Instead, they teach their youngsters early that all persons account for their lives and correct their own mistakes. When adolescents feel free to make their own decisions, they learn to make wise ones. They learn by careful forethought, trial and error, review and revision. Adolescents do not understand how to make effective, responsible decisions when the logical outcome disappears. They need real-world feedback in order to revise their thinking and make better decisions in the future.

Positive Peer Pressure

Maturity means acting with independence and responsibility. It means making thoughtful decisions and living successfully with the outcomes. Independence and responsibility do not arrive overnight. They take time and practice to develop. Peers can help each other in positive ways to build these qualities. In fact, the very closeness teens share with their friends and the pushing away from their families are signs of teens' beginning independence.

To act independently and responsibly, however, teens must first learn to know themselves, learn the rules of their larger society, learn how to make good decisions. They do these things with their friends in many ways.

Friends tell teens about themselves. In a group, teens can listen to and watch other people's ideas and values in action. They can watch their friends take schoolwork seriously and build strong academic skills, or they can watch their friends goof off and stop achieving well. They can watch their friends having relationships with one another, sometimes arguing, sometimes helping, sometimes telling the truth or sometimes bending it to meet their own needs. They can see their friends' views about dating, drugs and alcohol, and driving habits. They can observe how their friends act around other people in the school cafeteria, at basketball games, in the store downtown.

As they watch their friends, teens ask themselves, "Is this the way I would act in this situation? Is this what I believe? Is this what I want for myself?"

Many teens also talk openly and intimately with each other about what they believe and value, and they share the questions they have about meaning in their lives. Teens need to really know and understand themselves as persons. They need to know what matters to them and what is important to them right now as well as in the future if they are to make effective, satisfying, and responsible decisions as mature adults.

Friends tell teens what is normal, right, or appropriate. Young teens don't know how they are supposed to act in new situations in school, at the mall, or in their friends' homes. They want to fit in, act like everyone else, and not appear weird. They watch what their friends do and listen to what their friends say is the right way. Slowly, teens try out these new ways. Some feel comfortable. Some feel awkward at first but get easier with practice. Some bring the feeling, "This is not me!" and the attitude or behavior is tried once and then dropped. Over time, teens build the skills and self-confidence to act correctly and ably in many situations.

The more the skill and the greater the self-confidence, the more teens can make their own decisions about what ideas and behaviors are normal, right, or appropriate. As teens mature, the less need they have to depend on their friends' ideas about how to act. Skills and self-confidence lead to truly responsible independence.

Friends also let each other succeed. Groups of friends deal with right now, concrete issues of friendship, clothing, and activities. They can all meet each others' expectations. Meeting their friends' expectations feels good to young people. It gives them a sense of mastery, competence, and confidence. These qualities of "I can!" are positive contributors to independence and responsibility.

Finally, friends answers teens' questions about whether they are worthwhile and valuable people. Their parents have to love them, but their friends are with them because they want to be. Having a friend means that someone chooses to like you and to spend time with you. It means acceptance, belonging, and chances to be close to another person. Teens with friends feel lovable and worthwhile. They feel good about themselves. Teens who feel good about themselves want to achieve in positive ways. They want to make it as successful adults in the larger society. These teens are willing to learn and to pick themselves up from their mistakes and do a better job next time. Feeling worthwhile and valuable means having room to grow without being afraid of making mistakes. These teens are willing to make the best (rather than the fastest) decisions. Friendship is a vote of confidence that helps teens to learn the attitudes and skills that lead to independence and responsibility.

Conclusion

Adolescents have much to learn before reaching adult maturity. Independence and responsibility call for calm decision-making. They mean making mistakes, reviewing results closely, and finding improved answers in present disappointments. Independence means receiving here while giving there. It means gracefully accepting the truism that there is no free lunch.

Independence and responsibility require knowing themselves and taking charge of their behavior. It means developing the internal controls to become self-monitoring. It requires learning how to form individual opinions and how to solve problems. Becoming an adult demands building skills—personal, social, and vocational—that permit increasing mastery of their own lives.

At last, maturity means having the ability to be a good friend as well as a competent, independent individual. Sincerely caring for the others' well-being, showing empathy, trusting, laughing, or crying with friends mark strong relationships. Likewise, showing respect by allowing other people to make their own decisions and follow their personal values also signals vital relationships. Increasingly, friends begin to appreciate their differences in addition to their similarities. They initially come together for safety and support, but they stay together for respect, caring, and appreciation.

With maturity, "we" becomes me and you. Individuals understand and like themselves and their special uniqueness. They can choose to be separate or together, but the choosing remains the important factor. Now the group becomes a collection of separate persons who sometimes seek each other's company for a time and then leave for separate lives. Individuals cherish both aspects, the social and the private.

Index

A

abortion, teenage, 95
abuse, sexual, 100-101
acceptance
  lack of, 163
  by peers, 14, 18, 25, 28-29, 34, 52, 76,
    79-80, 125, 131, 147, 163, 183, 201
  rejecting, 35
  of self, 154, 156, 157, 161, 165, 169,
    170, 178, 183
accidents, alcohol-related, 55, 76
achievement, 57-83, 201
  drive for, 162
  of gifted, 148-149, 150, 155-156,
    159, 163, 182
activities
  boy-girl, 17, 33
  sexual, 93, 94, 161
  reasons for, 95-106, 110
  social, 57
  as symbols of maturity, 85
adolescence
  peer pressure in, 23-56
  as transition, 1-22
adventure, 58, 69-71, 85, 124
affection
  need for, 28, 133
  parental, 86
  of peers, 14
  sharing, 94
age, and peer pressure, 26-27
alcohol, 47, 50, 51-52, 80, 84-85,
  160, 195, 200
anger
  expressing through sex, 97, 110, 137
  expressing through suicide, 137
  at loss, 113, 114, 121, 128
  at parents' sexual problems, 135
  unexpressed, 79, 85, 105, 134
answers
  from peer group, 2, 31
  seeking, 25
anxiety, 7, 10, 28, 52

attitudes
  adult, 59
  building, 57, 83, 89
  changing, 42
  "normal," 13
  refining, 61, 110, 119
  sexual, 89, 91, 135, 137
Attribution Theory, 71-72, 191-192
automobile, as symbol of adulthood, 50

B

behaviors
  acceptable, 6, 19
  adult, 90, 91, 102, 125, 198
  aggressive, 90
  antisocial, 27-28, 39, 77, 80, 170
  changing, 15, 19, 42, 141
  exploratory, 89-95
  influenced by feelings, 114
  intrapersonal, 51
  justifying, 23
  of learning-disabled, 167-168
  normal, 13, 85, 90, 201
  parental influence on, 59
  self-destructive, 77, 141
  sexual, 60-61, 84-95, 114, 135, 137
  trying new, 25, 84-85, 86, 111, 119,
    132, 200
black adolescents, 172-181
block, to achievement, 63, 66, 169
body
  changes in, 4, 45, 86
  concerns about, 11-12

C

change
  accepting, 112, 126-127, 145
  fear of, 170
  physical, 4, 87
  psychological, 6
  as upsetting, 20
cheating, 67
choices
  considering, 108-109

making, 3, 31, 35, 36, 140, 184, 199
outcome of, 86, 185, 195
classes, special
for gifted, 155, 164-165
for learning-disabled, 171
clique, 15-18, 177
acceptable, 34
leadership, 27
clothes, and peer pressure, 44-46, 61, 80
153, 158, 183
conformity, 14, 25, 26, 35
contraception, 95, 96
counselor, peer, 52-53, 82
crowd, adolescent, 15-18

D

dating, 16-17, 60, 92, 99, 104, 105,
130, 200
parental, 135, 136
daydreaming, 43-44, 114
death, 112, 113, 115, 118, 120, 141, 145
decision-making, 1, 5, 9, 13, 19, 22, 52, 53,
81, 83, 85, 120, 147, 183, 184-185
avoiding, 26, 57, 86
five-step process of, 192-194
poor, 124, 186
depression, of loss, 138-139
development
group, 17
sexual, 85
differentness, 147, 182
of blacks, 172
of gifted, 152, 153, 155, 159
of learning-disabled, 165-166
discouragement, 74-76, 100, 174
divorce, 112, 113, 118, 120, 123, 131-137,
141, 145
double standard, 94
dress code, peer group, 12-13, 46
driving
drunk, 73
reckless, 84-85, 141, 195
as symbol of adulthood, 50-51, 185, 198
drug abuse, 47-49, 50, 55, 73, 76, 79, 84-85,
124, 139, 141, 160, 170, 195, 200

E

early adolescence, 3, 16, 40, 60
emotions, 8
of gifted, 150, 165
in loss, 121-125
empathy, 6, 19, 20, 38, 71, 165, 202

environment
interacting with, 2, 57
mastery of, 62, 73
understanding, 58
expectations
friends', 20, 178-179
of gifted, 149, 158, 163
group, 25, 31, 53, 93, 101, 102-103,
131, 156
rejecting, 35
low, 62
sexual, 12
social, 4-5, 6, 8-9, 10-11, 13, 91, 94, 184

F

face, saving, 71, 72, 129, 131, 163
failure
adolescent, 62-65
avoiding, 65-69, 71-72, 83, 129
fear of, 13, 175, 195
feelings of, 99-100
of learning-disabled, 169, 170
family
blended, 136-137
breakup of, 118-120
influence of, 28-29, 178
fantasizing, 43-44, 88, 89-90, 91
fear
about differentness, 183
acting out through sex, 137
at loss, 113, 121, 140
at parents' dating, 136
unexpressed, 79, 85
feelings
accepting, 121
becoming unimportant, 74
denying, 115-117, 128-129
expressing, 107-108, 123-124
fear of, 49
of gifted, 150, 165
let-down, 113
love/hate, 121-122, 134
positive, 52
sensitivity to, 148
friends
helping friends, 107-109, 142
keeping, 1, 86, 175, 196-197
making, 1, 27, 154, 169
peer group, 37-38
as security, 118
sensitivity of, 140

friendship
  broken, 112
  developing, 41
  need for, 79, 150
  offering, 39

G
gender
  identity, 85
  masking, 45
gifted adolescents, 147, 148-164, 172, 182
goals
  losing interest in, 74, 114, 175
  loss of, 113
  realistic, 67-68
  setting, 9-10, 111-112, 147, 181, 182
  uncertainty about, 25
  unmet, 35
  unrealistic, 65-66, 68
gossip, 41-43
Governor's School for the Gifted, 156
grief
  acceptance of, 115, 145
  emotions of, 113
guilt, feelings of, 49, 52, 109, 121, 123, 134

H
hand-holding, 90, 91, 92, 102

I
identity
  establishing, 13, 18, 57, 85, 86, 95,
    132, 151, 158
  group, 38, 52, 125
  and loss, 117-120
  racial, 179-180
  rejecting, 35
  sexual, 135
  uncertain, 26, 120
incentive, for success, 62, 63
incest, 100-101, 137
independence, 5, 13, 21, 25, 38, 47, 50, 52
  achieving, 57, 59, 77, 110, 118, 184-202
  linked with responsibility, 197-199
  loss of, 89
  need for, 80, 83, 85, 86
influence
  adult, 77
  denial of, 33, 35
  external, 34-36
  internal, 32, 35-36
  parental, 80
intercourse, sexual, 89, 91, 95, 102, 103

J
job, after-school, 5, 61, 62, 63

"Just Say No," 54-55
juvenile delinquency, 170, 183

L
late adolescence, 17-18
leadership, 60, 61, 153
  learning, 8, 19, 81-82
learning-disabled adolescents, 75, 147,
    165-171, 172, 182, 183
life-style
  alternative, 17
  peer group, 20, 185
loneliness
  of gifted, 152, 163, 165
  relief of, 20
  sex as escape from, 99, 101
  suicidal, 137
loss, adolescent, 111-145, 184
love, falling in, 87
loyalty, 6, 17, 20
  to ethnic group, 173
luck
  and achievement, 71
  and failure, 76, 174

M
mastery, personal, 5, 13, 15, 71, 121,
    191, 202
masturbation, 91, 95
middle adolescence, 3, 16, 60
minority-group adolescents, 147,
    172-181, 182, 183
mistakes
  learning from, 77, 194-196, 201
  teenagers', and parents, 20-22, 114
molestation, sexual, 100-101
moving, loss at, 112, 115-117, 145

N
needs
  for achievement, 58
  changing, 15
  emotional, 58, 83, 87
  meeting, 47, 53, 78-79
  unmet, 35

O
Operation Prom/Graduation, 55
opinions, forming, 189-191

P
parents
  reliance on, 46
  and teenagers, 20-22
  unconcerned, 28-29
peer group
  academic, 38, 39, 40, 42, 60, 61, 69,
    70, 76, 82, 158
  and achievement, 59-62

athletic, 38-39, 40, 69
avoidance of failure, 68-69
changes in, 15-18
creative, 40
image, 12, 43
misfits, 39-40
motivation to join, 27-28, 161, 175, 185
role of, 8-15, 158
as scapegoat, 76-80
and sexuality, 101-106
social, 38, 39, 40, 42, 60, 61, 70, 158
values, 18-20
power
    sex as proof of, 104-105, 110
    sense of, 118
pregnancy, adolescent, 95, 106
pressure
    on blacks, 174-181
    on gifted, 149
    internal, 52, 114
    negative, 54
    positive, 55, 76, 81-90, 102, 107, 109,
        143, 156, 164, 165, 171
    sex as escape from, 98-99, 101, 110
    social, 8, 10, 94
privacy
    invading, 90, 97
    loss of, 113
    need for, 4, 41
problem-solving, 5, 34, 53, 82-83,
    108-109, 132, 148, 194, 202
    poor, 124, 168
    sexual activity in, 97, 106-107
Project SMART, 82-83
puberty, 3, 45, 87, 95

R
rape, 100
Raspberry, William, 173
reassurance
    parental, 133
    from peer group, 2, 11, 26
    through sex, 160-161
rebellion, sex as, 97, 101
rejection, fear of, 28, 103
relationship
    boy-girl, 16, 43, 61, 125-131, 143-144
    black-white, 175-176
    building, 3, 5-6, 40, 57, 86, 93-94, 169, 200
    end of, 125-131
    heterosexual, 6, 17
    intimate, 15-16, 38, 46, 86, 93, 104, 136
    mature, 87
    meaningful, 111-112, 119
    physical, 87
    sexual, 88-89, 95-96, 98, 102
remarriage, parental, 131-137
responsibility
    accepting, 8, 35, 36, 120, 151
    avoiding, 37, 85

learning, 50, 57, 61, 184-202
linked with independence, 197-199
romance
    broken, 125-131, 143-145
    and peer group influence, 43
    and sex, 87
rules
    group, 31-32, 35, 37, 43, 101, 183
    inconsistently applied, 28
    parental, 198
    social, 25, 199
rumor, 41, 43, 82

S
scapegoat, peer pressure as, 76-80
secrets, as adult behavior, 41-42
security, loss of, 112
self-assurance, 38, 119, 159, 178, 191
    lack of, 169
self-awareness, 51, 52, 57
    developing, 89, 110
    lack of, 157, 163
self-blame, 26, 30
self-confidence, 20, 29, 30, 40, 49,
    62, 64, 81, 179, 191
    lack of, 121, 131, 133-134, 140, 145,
        163, 183, 195
self-definition, 3-4, 25, 57, 86, 87, 89,
    96, 118, 151
self-esteem, 13, 14, 20, 42, 57, 58, 71
self-knowledge, 178-179, 192, 199, 200, 202
self-respect, 78
self-understanding, 149, 151, 157, 161,
    165, 170, 172
sex
    as alternative to relationship, 104
    premarital, 93, 94-95
    rejection of, 135-136
    as symbol of maturity, 96, 136, 160
sexuality
    adolescent, 84-110
    adult, 88-89
    emerging, 43, 45
    imitating adult, 61
    parental, 135
skills
    adult, 50
    building, 2, 22, 57, 81, 83, 119, 125,
        184, 191-192
    helping, 53, 83
    intellectual, 7-8, 148, 183, 192
    interpersonal, 61, 183, 192
    leadership, 30
    listening, 53, 82, 142-143, 177
    practicing, 3, 192
    reasoning, 190-191
    social, 8, 17, 19, 25, 40, 151, 192
stepfamily, 122-123, 132, 136-137
Students Against Drunk Driving (SADD), 55
suicide, 137-143

of gifted, 163-164
sex as form of, 99-100
support
emotional, 5, 9, 14, 27-28
financial, 5, 9
group, 23, 25, 52, 65, 79, 109, 120, 133, 140, 154, 157, 159, 169, 175, 183
rejecting, 35
parental, 46, 154, 198
social, 15, 27
telephone, as adult symbol, 46-47, 198
tension
emotional, 7, 34, 49, 51, 89, 123-124
group, 82
physical, 88, 95
relief of, 20
sexual, 136-137
thoughts
abstract, 21, 167, 192
denial of, 33
influences on, 24, 79
"normal," 13
organizing, 7-8
reflective, 51, 77, 189
sexual, 88
trust, 6, 86, 90, 94, 111, 202

U
unisex clothing, 12, 45

V
values, 28, 78, 91
black vs. white, 172-173, 176, 179-180
changing, 1
choosing, 21, 85, 89, 93
parental, 93, 118, 132
peer group, 18-20, 24
sexual, 102, 137
societal, 38
testing, 110-111

W
warnings, suicidal, 140-143
Washington Area Improvisational Teen Theatre (WAITT), 106-107
worth, personal, 14-15, 25, 26, 52, 65, 68, 72, 110, 125, 137

Y
Youth Alcohol Abuse Prevention Project (YAAPP), 55